God-Size Your Church is a must-read for all church leaders who desire to be obedient to Christ's commissioning of the Church. It will challenge and provoke you to lead your congregation to the next level by increasing its influence in your community and having a God-sized impact for the kingdom.

Morton Wyatt, Lead Pastor, Life Change Church, Chowchilla, CA (average worship attendance 150)

John has combined his passion for understanding different church growth models with his personal success as a church planter and coach to produce this practical, information-packed book. Thank you, John, for taking the conversation one step further.

Dan Axtell, Pastor, Restoration Life Community Church, Sacramento, CA (average worship attendance 250)

God-Size Your Church is a tremendously helpful and inspiring resource. . . . Reading it was a refreshing and "vision expanding" experience. Dr. John Jackson has challenged me to super-size my vision, and think bigger, even as I serve in a small community.

Mark O. Wilson, Senior Pastor, Hayward Wesleyan Church, Hayward, WI (average worship attendance 650)

In *God-Size Your Church*, John Jackson delivers more than just principles to swell the size of your Sunday attendance. Instead, he gives practical advice and wisdom from years of experience that will enable church leaders to grow mature disciples who seriously engage and impact their communities and world for the sake of the kingdom.

Dr. Tim Brown, Senior Pastor, First Baptist Church of Clovis, CA (average worship attendance 900)

GOD-SIZE YOUR CHURCH

GOD-SIZE YOUR CHURCH

maximizing your impact

john jackson

Transforming lives through God's Word

Transforming lives through God's Word

Biblica provides God's Word to people through translation, publishing and Bible engagement in Africa, Asia Pacific, Europe, Latin America, Middle East, and North America. Through its worldwide reach, Biblica engages people with God's Word so that their lives are transformed through a relationship with Jesus Christ.

Biblica Publishing
We welcome your questions and comments.

1820 Jet Stream Drive, Colorado Springs, CO 80921 USA
www.Biblica.com

God-Size Your Church
ISBN-13: 978-1-60657-107-1

Copyright © 2008, 2011 by John Jackson

13 12 11 / 6 5 4 3 2 1

A catalog record for this book is available through the Library of Congress.

Printed in the United States of America

CONTENTS

ACKNOWLEDGMENTS

I want to thank and recognize the many mentors who have shaped my life along the way, though I know it is impossible to mention everyone. My parents and my family have continually taught me with love and wisdom. I was privileged to have many teachers, many examples, and many friends along the way. Pastors and writers mentored me without ever knowing it. Men like John Maxwell, Rick Warren, Bill Hybels, Jack Hayford, Andy Stanley, Ed Young Jr., Jimmy Evans, Robert Morris, Brady Boyd, and a host of others have sown seeds into my life from up close and from afar. I once listed my favorite books and tried to stop at thirty but could not. Friends like Glenn, Ray, Scott, Tom, Dane, David, Tim, Andy, and others contribute to my life in a way that is hard to measure. My current teammates at Bayside Church are making my life richer and more complete every week. My former colleagues on staff and in leadership at LifePoint Church (www.lifepointnv.com) have written and shaped (and are shaping!) this story more than they will ever know. Paul Borden and the team at Growing Healthy Churches (www.growinghealthychurches.org) have helped us extend and "ripple" our story and my contribution to others. The team at Biblica has continued to be a rich source of encouragement and focus. So, anything good you see in here came from a stream of sources that can't be named. Any flaws you find in this book are mine alone.

As always, my wife, Pam, and my children, Jennifer, Dena, Rachel, Joshua, and Harrison, are at the center of my world next to Jesus. To them, I owe an amazing debt of gratitude for their love and care in my life. I want to acknowledge that Jesus Christ is the Lord of the church and of my life, and ultimately, anything of value here comes from his throne and his heart. My prayer is for you to God-size his role and impact in your life and the lives of those around you.

FOREWORD

I recently heard a pastor describe his church by saying, "We aren't trying to build a *megachurch*—we're trying to build a *healthy* church."

When I heard that, I thought, *Why can't the Christian church be both?* When did growth and health become mutually exclusive? Shouldn't the Christian church be both growing *and* healthy? Shouldn't thriving churches major in both evangelism *and* discipleship? Why can't a congregation have both size *and* significance?

That's why this book is such a breath of fresh air. As I read *God-Size Your Church*, I thought, *It's about time!* A leader among leaders, John Jackson has delivered what I think is his most valuable book, which makes clear that business as usual just isn't cutting it! Need convincing? Ask yourself a few innocent questions:

- Why is the rate of population growth far outpacing the church's rate of growth?
- Why are 87 percent of Protestant churches stagnant or declining?

- Why did 50 percent of all churches in the year 2000 fail to add a single new member through conversion?
- Why are Christian churches losing their teenagers?
- Why does the local McDonald's often know more about its community than the local church?
- Why do local churches often make zero difference in their communities?
- Why are many pastors described best by the phrase *faithful but discouraged*?

If you are asking questions like these, this book is for you! Years of coaching churches and church leaders make John uniquely equipped to offer both inspiration and practical principles that will help churches of every size! This is a must-read book that will energize and equip leaders to build thriving churches—churches that are growing *and* healthy!

What's at stake? Everything. Every church has scores of people needing a passionate leader to inspire them to God-first, God-honoring living, and every community has thousands of people disconnected from Christ needing a high-octane church to demonstrate and deliver the good news.

My prayer is that God will use this book to light fires in you and your church that will never go out but will burn like a beacon of hope in your community.

November 2010
Ray Johnston
Pastor, Bayside Church
Granite Bay, California

INTRODUCTION

"**D**o you want to supersize your drink and fries for just forty cents more?"

Supersizing a drink and fries seems reasonable to our fast-food culture. But what if I asked you if you wanted a regular or a supersized church? And what if I asked you about supersizing your church's impact? Before you answer these two questions, let me ask you one more. Does a bigger church always make a bigger impact?

We often measure church impact only from a numerical standpoint—how many programs, how many members, how big a campus. However, numbers alone do not tell the whole story. There are many more dimensions to what God is doing in your church and community than simple numbers. I believe that *God*-sizing your impact is far more important than striving to supersize it. Rather than focusing exclusively on higher numbers, we can focus on making a real difference in our churches and communities.

Your church is poised to make a God-sized impact. If you are passionate about fulfilling the Great Commission—and the fact that you are reading this book is a good indication that you are!—then you want to maximize your church's influence. God has given each of us an opportunity to lead and participate in a kingdom adventure. Our challenge is to fulfill the divine mandate he has given us. The apostle Paul said it this way: "Do you not know that in a race all the runners run, but only one gets the prize? Run in such a way as to get the prize. Everyone who competes in the games goes into strict training. They do it to get a crown that will not last, but we do it to get a crown that will last forever" (1 Corinthians 9:24–25).

Let's begin a journey of discovery. Many times we have come to believe that our communities cannot be reached for Christ because of the hardness of people's hearts. Although that may be true in specific cases, another fundamental reality is often also at work. Often we reach our limit of influence because we demand that our churches be structured a certain way, from pastoral care to ministry to education. Our journey of discovery will bring us to the edge of a vital question: Is it more important for our churches to meet our needs or to transform our communities? God-sizing our churches isn't about whether they are big or small—it's about whether our strategic vision and values match the heart of God.

I write this with great personal passion. I believe that God wants our churches to reach more people for Jesus Christ, to establish and secure them in their faith, and to equip them for kingdom work in the world. God longs for lost people to know him and for saved people to share him with others: "So then, just as you received Christ Jesus as Lord, continue to live your lives in him, rooted and built up in him, strengthened in the faith as you were taught, and overflowing with thankfulness" (Colossians 2:6–7).

Researcher Dave Olsen, in his book *The American Church in Crisis*, estimates that more than 90 percent of American churches are either at a plateau or declining compared to the population growth in their communities. Rather than us giving in to despair however, I think that God is even now beginning to show us his vision for the future. God is right now beginning a movement of healthy, externally focused churches in smaller areas that are making a God-sized difference in their local communities. As my friend Mark Wilson reminds readers on his blog (www.revitalizeyourchurch.blogspot.com), "Your church can touch the world, regardless of your location. You can make a big difference right where you are!"

Imagine moving beyond the business-as-usual impact so many churches currently accept—not to a supersized impact concerned only with numbers, but a God-sized impact that transforms churches and communities of every size with the good news of God's Son through the power of God's Spirit. All over this country, churches of every size believe that they can make a God-sized difference.

What about you?

chapter 1

DREAMING GOD-SIZED DREAMS

I n 1996, at a snow-covered church campground in Greenlake, Wisconsin, I heard God ask me a question: *Will you dare to dream big dreams for me?*

My first response was *No!*

I had been wrestling with God for quite some time about my future in ministry, but on that snowy day, I was reading the story of church planter Rick Warren in *The Purpose-Driven Church.* I thought I was quite familiar with the story, given that we had lived in Southern California when Saddleback was beginning. That day, God seemed to be speaking into my heart, and a dream of a local church that would reach unchurched people and change the world started to form. My initially icy response to God melted as the fire of passion began to burn in my heart.

Many of us are initially reluctant to dream big. Intuitively, we know that dreaming big leads to big changes in our lives and ministries. Big change requires risk as we exchange security for the unknown. Yet I am convinced that God is asking many of you the same question he asked me in 1996: *Will you dare to dream big dreams for me?*

Please do me two favors before you continue reading. First, dream a big dream of what God could do through you and your church if there were no obstacles in the way. Five years from now, if there were no limitations on finances, leadership, facilities, or programs, how could God change the world through your local church? Picture it. What would worship look like? How would evangelism, discipleship, fellowship, and ministry take place? What life changes would people experience? Look at every ministry dimension with as much clarity as you can.

Second, take every dimension of your five-year dream, and multiply it by a factor of ten. Let your spirit, heart, and mind soar as you consider what God could do that would be *ten times your grandest dream*. When you envision that, you'll *just* be starting to grasp what God is able to do. When we dare to dream big dreams for God, and then allow God to work in and through us with his wisdom, love, and power, we're beginning to God-size!

I'd like to tell you a story of a God-sized dream in action. My friend Mike Holba pastors Ripon Community Church in Ripon, Wisconsin. Listen to the ways God is working in and through his church to make a God-sized difference:

> The first time I experienced a God-sized dream coming to fruition, I was planting my first church in Ripon, Wisconsin. As we drove into the small town of Ripon, I never would have guessed that we were about to exchange our minivan for a front-row seat on God's roller coaster.

When asked to describe our experiences planting a church here in Ripon, I often say, "It's like having front-row seats for a miracle." At least that's how I describe it on the good days. On the other days, when I am still trying to figure out what God is up to, I often say, "It's like we're in the front row of a roller coaster and God is operating the ride. It's thrilling, exhilarating, and sometimes scary! But, because we have faith in the Operator, we know we'll be safe."

I would have never predicted that this seven-thousand-person town would see so many miracles, that so much would be possible. But God in his ultimate wisdom and holiness did. We began our church with no people, almost no money, and very little experience. All we had was a simple desire to try to determine what God wanted, and then do it. Genesis 6:22, "Noah did everything just as God commanded him," became our special passage. It worked pretty well for Noah, so why not us?

We began making plans and dreaming of what God might do. But I am slightly embarrassed to admit that even though I am a dreamer and a goal setter, my dreams were way too "small town" for this tiny community. God's were huge!

With God at the controls, we simply targeted people who were turned off by church, but not by God, and we went from five people to one hundred in six months. Average attendance rose to two hundred during the next six months, and to four hundred over the next few years.

At our first baptism service, we baptized sixty-five people in nearby Green Lake. The water was so cold that my surgically repaired knee was numb by the time I got out of the water. After five years, we have now baptized almost 3 percent of the city's population!

Two hundred people participate in our small groups, and we now provide food to nearly four hundred people each month through our Thrift Store/Food Pantry ministry. We have also planted two daughter churches in other towns similar to our own.

The miracles that we have witnessed are too numerous to list. Hundreds of people have now dedicated their lives to following Jesus. The story of "Joanne" is an exemplary testament to God's power in the life of anyone willing to open the door when Jesus knocks.

A few months before the church launched, Joanne sent me an e-mail saying:

"I am one of those people who is disenchanted with the church. I want to choose how much time I spend with church and do not want to be prodded into Bible studies, etc. I don't want people being judgmental and have not yet found a church that does not make judgments. I don't want a church to tell me how much money I should be giving. I don't want to feel like an outsider in a clique of Bible thumpers. I need a minister whom I can feel comfortable baring my soul to if need be. Do I sound hopeless—or like the average disenchanted church person? Please drop me an e-mail. I will not be the least bit insulted if you tell me that I am climbing the wrong cross, and this church will not meet my expectations."

It might sound crazy, but I was so excited reading that e-mail! People like Joanne are the reason we plant churches. She was exactly who I was looking for, far from God but full of potential. Joanne has since given her life to Jesus, been baptized, and has invited many, many people to attend. Her brother died recently, and with my blessing, she conducted his memorial service herself.

After a very passionate message, she concluded her thoughts with the following statement:

"I don't know all of your beliefs. I know that everyone is in a different place and that's okay. Faith is a journey. Sometimes we stay on the road, sometimes there is a detour, and sometimes we're just lost. The important thing is that we eventually reach our destination. I believe that Jesus died for our sins. God's love for us is not earned; it is freely given."

Considering her first e-mail, I would call Joanne's conversion a miracle. I was dreaming human-sized big dreams, but God wanted to multiply the impact of our church on this small town in ways I never would have thought possible. We have actually lived out Ephesians 3:20 over these last five years in tiny Ripon, Wisconsin, and there are now hundreds of people here who can quote that verse and say with belief, "To God be the glory," because of what he has done here.

Now that's what I call God-sizing!

Business as usual won't cut it anymore. The church has been a bedrock foundation of Western society for hundreds of years, but today the church is standing on the edge of irrelevance. We need a fresh, bold, articulate vision for ministry that can be played out in local communities across the country, regardless of their size. George Barna goes one step further when he says, "Let's cut to the chase. After nearly two decades of studying Christian churches in America, I'm convinced that the typical church as we know it today has a rapidly expiring shelf life."[1]

Churches across America, large and small, are grappling with barriers to their growth and questioning their future. Some researchers have suggested the United States experiences a net loss of 2,500 churches per year![2] When local churches are forced to close their doors, they certainly can't fulfill the Great Commission of Matthew 28:18–20 in their local communities. If business as usual is resulting in fewer and fewer churches each year—and less discipleship and less evangelism, too—it's time to do something different!

My passion in this book is to equip you to hear from God about your ministry and to go where he tells you to go. God-sizing is *not* about making your church a big church. It is about fulfilling the kingdom agenda of God in your community for his glory. God wants our churches to grow in order to reach new people for him and to influence our culture for Christ!

chapter 2

IS GOD-SIZING BIBLICAL?

What if, in the space of five years, your church doubled in attendance, baptisms increased by fourfold, annual giving increased tenfold, and you completed a building campaign in which you financed the entire project with cash? By all conventional measurements you would be a pastoral success, and your church would clearly be a God-sized church, right?

But what if, during that same time period, the rates of divorce, suicide, and alcoholism in your community did not change, total attendance in all churches of your community remained the same, and your members, when surveyed, did not love or follow Christ with any more depth or passion?

Pastoral success is about rightly understanding, pursuing, and achieving God's vision for your ministry. God-sizing your church means hearing and pursuing that definition of pastoral success, even when tempted to pursue more conventional definitions of success. For most of us, beginning to consider what God has for our ministries causes us to lean forward toward the future and grasp what a church would look like that prevails against the forces of evil in our respective communities. Thinking about a local church that prevails against the presence of hell in its community is energizing.

However, most pastoral leaders feel the opposite in our churches. We've watched, participated in, or led ailing churches that could use a strong dose of hope—or even shock treatment! Discouragingly, we are clear that God is calling us to lead these churches toward health and vitality, yet there doesn't seem to be a path away from their flaws and limits. Perhaps you wonder why your church seems hollow, despite its large size, or wondered for years whether you are really having the impact in the community that attendance numbers seemed to indicate. Over time, you've pondered whether small, stagnant churches can ever become healthy, and whether larger churches actually make a significant difference for Christ in their communities.

What if we could plant seeds in such a way that the soil would bear thirty-, sixty-, or hundredfold returns? These are the dreams of church leaders who want to reach their community through God-sized, high-impact churches. *High-impact churches break through spiritual, social, and leadership barriers to establish new churches and new ministries and reach large numbers of new people for Christ. High-impact churches confront the law of inertia and the reality of human lethargy with a passionate, purposeful pursuit of God's plan for evangelism in their areas.*

Dreaming is fine, but then we must walk into the reality of our world. According to the Great Commission Research Network (formerly the American Society for Church Growth, www.ascg.org), there is no county in America that has a higher percentage of churched persons today than a decade ago. I have personally heard C. Peter Wagner say it another way: "There are more churches on birth control than people!"[3] We believe that many churches have now broken that statistic in our county, and we hear stories from other churches that are having a similar God-sized impact. (Read the story of the church we planted in northern Nevada in the next chapter.)

So, why would anyone consider investing his or her life in the ministry of the local church? Only two phrases make the opportunity worth considering: *Jesus Christ* and *Great Commission.* Jesus Christ, as our Lord and Savior, not only gave us the Great Commission assignment of reaching and teaching people, but also gave us the vehicle with which to travel that road. In the local church one can know Christ and grow in him—and one must reach out with that love and knowledge into the surrounding community. We must be clear about the fact that Jesus has commissioned us to go into our particular communities and make known the good news. Reaching the lost people in our neighborhoods is *our* job. As Perry Noble says, "We should make it hard to get to hell from our zip code!"[4]

Jesus said, "All authority in heaven and on earth has been given to me. Therefore go and make disciples of all nations, baptizing them in the name of the Father and of the Son and of the Holy Spirit, and teaching them to obey everything I have commanded you. And surely I am with you always, to the very end of the age" (Matthew 28:18–20). That imperative, known as the Great Commission, is the defining purpose of the church of Jesus Christ. To fulfill God's game plan for ministry, we need to make the Great Commission front and center in all we do. Churches with a God-sized vision for high-impact ministry in their communities are fueled with passion for reaching people who are not in relationship with Jesus Christ.

Most of us would not argue with the notion that the Great Commission is at the center of the ministry of Jesus. It is true that we recognize the call for us, his followers, to follow that commission and reach lost people. At the same time, there are so many competing activities and possible areas of focus for the local church that the Great Commission is often pushed to the side. However, a healthy, thriving church will always have the Great Commission as an integral part of its DNA. Put in the negative, no church can be healthy or thrive if it fails to keep the Great Commission front and center in everything it does. We cannot fake the "heartbeat" of our vision. We can fake sermons, polite pastoral visits, and fund-raising appeals; but we cannot fake the single, animating vision that shapes everything else we do. Pastors and church leaders need to live and breathe this vision if it has any hope of spreading to the rest of the church and into the community. A leader's heart is like the center of a still pond: when a God-given vision for the lost drops into it, the ripples cannot help but spread, wider and wider, to the very edge of the pond. When you ache for your community, your church will ache with you.

Unless key leaders in your ministry have made the soul-gripping decision to be an outreach-based church, taking care of those already inside the fold will always take precedence over reaching the lost in your community, One experienced pastor says it this way: "The church of our time and our place is largely inwardly focused. It has lost sight of the world outside its walls. Which is to say, the church has also lost sight of the God who works in and loves the world. And that is a genuine tragedy." [5]

Let's put the primary issue in God-sizing your church on the table: size. Is bigger necessarily better? *No!* We want to move beyond mere numbers. A God-sized church is a place where people are consistently being reached for Christ on the campus *and* in the community. As people are being reached, they are being transformed and enabled, through the power of the Spirit, to reach even more people. God-sized churches, regardless of the absolute number of the persons attending weekend services, are passionate to see lost people found, saved people grow, hurting people healed, and all people use their spiritual gifts for the glory of God. That is a God-sized church—and if that's not biblical, then we're all in trouble!

God-sized churches have a passion to see this biblical passage lived out in their midst:

> As for you, you were dead in your transgressions and sins, in which you used to live when you followed the ways of this world and of the ruler of the kingdom of the air, the spirit who is now at work in those who are disobedient. All of us also lived among them at one time, gratifying the cravings of our flesh and following its desires and thoughts. Like the rest, we were by nature deserving of wrath. But because of his great love for us, God, who is rich in mercy, made us alive with Christ even when we were dead in transgressions—it is by grace you have been saved. And God raised us up with Christ and seated us with him in the heavenly realms in Christ Jesus, in order that in the coming ages he might show the incomparable riches of his grace, expressed in his kindness to us in Christ Jesus.

For it is by grace you have been saved, through faith—and this not from yourselves, it is the gift of God—not by works, so that no one can boast. For we are God's handiwork, created in Christ Jesus to do good works, which God prepared in advance for us to do. (Ephesians 2:1–10)

As we see people transferred from the kingdom of darkness to the kingdom of light, the name of God will be lifted up in our communities. People will be drawn to him through our churches, through our witness in the world, and through the power of changed lives. That is biblical, and it is what energizes leaders to dare to dream big—to God-size their churches!

One step you can take to God-size your church is to research your community. National statistics can be compelling, and church leaders do need to be familiar with the broad cultural trends in our country. However, local statistics are a vital part of the ministry plan of any healthy church. God-sized churches are high-impact churches in part because of their understanding of who lives and works around them, and what those particular people want and need. There are a number of good sites for demographic information; I have found http://www.epodunk.com/demographics/ to be particularly helpful. See how many of these questions you can answer for your community:

- What is the unchurched population in your community?
- By what percentage has the church population in your community increased or decreased over the past ten years? How does that compare to the increase or decrease in the general population?

- What is the church-to-population ratio in your community? What was it twenty years ago?
- How many churches has your community gained in the last three years? How many churches has it lost?
- Read Matthew 28:18–20. If your church has a vision or purpose statement, how does it incorporate the ideas of the Great Commission? As you start a new church, how will you incorporate a Great Commission mindset in those statements?

chapter 3

THE LIFEPOINT CHURCH STORY: VERSIONS 1.0, 2.0, AND 3.0

I f you dream of your church becoming God-sized, your dream must begin in the heart of God and catch fire in yours. I am praying and believing for you that you will have *his* vision for your ministry and your area. Whatever size church God is calling you to lead, it will come from his heartbeat and passion to see people connected to him. Until you catch a God-sized dream and ride the wave of that vision, you won't know what he has in store for you and your church.

During our first year at LifePoint Church (then named Carson Valley Christian Center or CVC), a man came up to me at one of our training events. He said, "I've listened to you, and I've watched what you're doing here. It doesn't look like you have a plan B if your strategy to reach the community fails." That man was a shrewd observer. I told him, "You're exactly right. We're completely committed to our vision, sink or swim."

From the beginning, we determined to trust God for great things. We didn't *think* insignificantly, we didn't *believe* insignificantly, and we didn't *behave* insignificantly. I went to meetings of the chamber of commerce and told them our dream was that our church would make a significant difference in the community. The risk was that I'd be laughed out of town after a couple of years if that didn't happen. The potential reward, however, was God-sized!

The clear vision for our church wasn't developed in a vacuum. God brought together a wonderful group of people who sacrificed time, money, and energy to invest their lives in reaching this area of Nevada for Christ. We all risked a lot. Now, after completing our ministry there in northern Nevada (we transitioned to my successor after twelve years of ministry), I believe we are seeing what God intended when he first birthed the vision in our hearts. Here is a little of our story:

I was born and raised in the home of an American Baptist pastor and his wife in Southern California during the 1960s and 1970s. Throughout my childhood, people patted me on the head and told me, "You're going to be a pastor just like your dad when you grow up." I'd grit my teeth and think, *Not if I can help it!* I wanted to be a professional baseball player, but at the age of fifteen I had a crisis when I realized that I wasn't good enough to go pro.

The next six months were a searching time that culminated in a very clear call from God at age sixteen to pastoral ministry. I met the girl who was soon to be my wife, turned eighteen in July 1979, married Pamela in August of that same year, and became a youth pastor at the First Baptist Church of Buena Park in September. I left Buena Park to become a youth pastor at Oxnard First Baptist Church (OFB) in January 1981. This church was to become formative in my life, even though the experience was a roller coaster ride! A master's degree from Fuller Seminary in June 1983 was followed by a PhD in educational administration from the University of California in June 1986. OFB went through an uproar the next year, which, after a long and painful process, resulted in my becoming the twenty-six-year-old acting senior pastor in late 1987 and then permanent senior pastor in mid-1988.

The years that I served at OFB are some of the sweetest and most painful of my over thirty years in ministry. Much growth happened, and yet there was lingering pain from the church difficulties of the earlier years. In October 1992, I was chosen to be the executive minister of the American Baptist Churches of the Pacific Southwest (ABCPSW, now Transformation Ministries; see www.transmin.org). ABCPSW was the largest mission-giving region in the country, but it was in a terrible financial and confidence crisis. Baptisms had plummeted, and the churches were not confident about the future. While working there, I began to wonder what solutions were available to help failing churches flourish, and I kept feeling an itch to leave.

LifePoint 1.0

In March 1996, God began to stir my heart toward planting a church for people who believe *church* is irrelevant to their lives but *God* isn't. On October 16, 1996, I resigned as the executive minister for the ABCPSW. Pam and I felt certain that God was calling us to plant a church in northern Nevada, where only 5 percent of the population attended church on a given weekend. The call seemed certain, but the circumstances were odd. I had lived my entire life in suburban Southern California with millions of people. Northern Nevada—where we were heading—was a rurban (rural becoming urban) environment with only 100,000 people within thirty miles of our church plant.

I knew that God wanted us to develop a high-impact church that would quickly break through growth and community penetration barriers, but there were no outreach-focused churches with membership of more than three hundred in our sphere of influence. Our experience with the existing churches is that they were inwardly focused and content to let the unreached remain unreached. To break this cultural cycle, we would need a team of committed people, sufficient financial backing, and God's amazing power—but we had no people, no money, and no clear indication of *how* God would do what we had come to believe he would do. I had experienced many churches imploding in their early lives because the leadership was insufficient for the ministry needs, and I prayed especially for a group of passionate leaders to emerge. God answered this prayer in a specific and tangible way.

My brother Gene and his wife, Barbara, committed early on to be part of the leadership team for the church plant. They had to move, leave a large church they loved (Eastside Christian Church in Fullerton), and sell Gene's business. Roy and Tracy Conover received our letter and told us they had been praying for a specific mission assignment. Both of them had participated in our youth ministry in Oxnard, had served on short-term mission trips, and had been part of a church plant (with some pain!) from Oxnard First Baptist. Not only were they called to join us and sell their home and quit their jobs, but it turned out they knew someone living in Carson Valley! Jacque and Cheri-Li Negrete joined us as soon as we moved here; they had actually participated in a church plant that we had done while I was the senior pastor of a previous church. The first leadership team of CVC was born: eight adults and twelve children made up the birthing coaches for the ministry.

Many stories of our early years remember the sacrifices of people from our Christmas card list—yes, we wrote the dreaded missionary letter, asking our friends and family for their support! Retired family friends, then in their nineties and living on a fixed income, gave fifty dollars per month to a church they would never see in order to reach people they would never know this side of heaven. A young couple in their thirties living in Spain with the U. S. Navy Seabees gave twenty dollars per month after receiving our letter. More than fifty other people gave amounts ranging from ten to two hundred dollars each month. Every time a letter came in the mail, it was a reminder of God's grace at work in his people. It was also a sobering reminder of our accountability for God's work at LifePoint Church.

Shortly after arriving in Carson Valley in April 1997, we began to plant the church. At least I think we did—boy, was I confused! I left a busy office and a busy schedule to move to a new area with no relationships and no office. I remember sitting in the guesthouse on our property, which was used as command central for the church. I had a game plan on paper, and I had big dreams, but I had no people! How could a God-sized church be established with no people? One day I spent an hour with my neighbor (an unbeliever), hanging out and talking. Then I left his home, saying, "I've got to get to work." God stopped me cold in my tracks. He said, *What do you think you have been doing?* Some church planter I was turning out to be.

After several months of getting settled, the four families that had moved to Carson Valley began meeting in a home group and developing relationships. Relationship building often meant going to the country store down the street (its owners now attend our church), hanging around the post office or local McDonald's, and talking with repair people who would come to our houses during the move-in process.

We spent a great deal of time in prayer and sharing those first few months. We had challenged people to become "Faith Promise Partners," and those living outside Carson Valley had committed more than two thousand hours of prayer per month, while those in the core team also committed many hours of prayer within the early months of the church. Determined to hold a barbecue at our home in July 1997, we invited every person we knew—the total was about fifty people, including out-of-town relatives! A second barbecue a month later drew eighty-five people. Each time we shared the vision for a new church, we sensed that God was stirring up a number of hearts. Practically, however, we still had no church and no people, and we were four months in.

Other than gathering for Bible study, we committed to worship together at local churches. We wanted to build a positive relationship with the churches, hoping that we could develop friends and partners in ministry. It had been my hope not to start a Sunday gathering until about three or four months before our February 1998 launch. As it turned out, most local churches in our area were uncomfortable with us attending. (It seemed clear that they were more threat sensitive than I had anticipated.)

As it turned out then, we began to meet together as a core group on the last Sunday of July in 1997. We met at a Lazer Tag amusement facility with about twenty-five people. We started to meet each Sunday with one condition: *no non-Christians would be invited to these gatherings.* They were core-group meetings, not outreach events. We were clear still that we were launching a church, so no non-Christians allowed . . . yet!

During this time, God opened a miraculous door, and we were able to purchase thirty-nine acres of property in our target geographical area at a price well below the market price at that time.

Though we had about thirty-five people participating regularly by August, many of them had never been in a larger church, and I knew they really needed to see an example to grasp the concept. So, in September, we visited Bayside Church near Sacramento, with twenty-three of our people. The senior pastor, Ray Johnston, gave us thirty valuable minutes in a local pizza parlor and answered questions. We took home a high-impact idea: hold preview services to reach potential core-group members, and do pre-evangelism in the community. On the two-hour ride home, we decided that our first preview would be three weeks later. (By the way, I now work with Ray at Bayside to help other churches impact their communities.)

Our first preview service, in September 1997, started an awe-inspiring pattern. We had 145 people in attendance, and 12 of them prayed to receive Christ. Our first Discovery 101 class was held that day, with 47 attendees. For three weeks, we met in a casino/hotel in Minden and then moved to a Carson City casino, where we stayed four months. We had preview services in October (175 people) and November (202 people); each time more than 20 people joined what we called our launch team, and some people prayed to receive Christ. Discovery 101 classes were taught in the afternoon after each preview service, and we followed up with Discovery 201 and 301 classes. All services and classes were held in a section of the casino ballroom.

Then, in the eight weeks prior to our launch, we intentionally pushed our people and community toward the launch date of February 22, 1998. One hundred adults were on our team, and sixty-five of them had a specific service role in the life of the church. An enterprise only goes public once, so we went with all our hearts and souls. We used creative direct mail, newspaper inserts, posters, personal handout cards, and a variety of other outreach mechanisms to contact homes and businesses. We told all of our people that they were at "Cape Canaveral—we're launching a church instead of a rocket, and what you do in your role can make the difference in the entire project."

By January 1998, we located a warehouse facility, and our local county affirmed our leasing of the facility on one condition: we had to secure a building permit at a cost of $100,000 and promise to complete our new facility on our land in twelve months. We pursued every alternative avenue, but it seemed clear that was to be our pathway. (As an aside, I *do not* recommend building or buying anything in the first three to five years of a church launch, unless it happens to be God's provision and plan, as it was for LifePoint Church.) In less than thirty days, we renovated 10,000 square feet of the empty 40,000-square-foot warehouse. One hundred adults and forty-five children assembled in the building one week before Launch Sunday.

On Launch Sunday, 424 people attended, and there were more than twenty decisions for Christ. We were ecstatic! The next eighteen months were a journey on which God continually stretched our faith and vision. At our first Easter service, 674 people attended. We added two services in June 1998, and more than 1,300 people joined us for Easter services of 1999. We raised just over $300,000 toward the new building in 1998 and 1999, and we moved to our property in an 18,000-square-foot multipurpose building in October of 1999 because of pressure from our county to move out of our temporary buildings. We had a facility and land valued at $2.7 million upon move-in, and we owed $2.4 million. (Again, I do not recommend this!) We borrowed heavily from friends in ministry and were awed at how God kept meeting needs. Our key leaders sacrificed greatly to see these steps take place. Does size matter? At this point, it seemed like every indication was that we had launched a "successful" church by every dimension. I think we did, but trouble was just starting to brew.

CVC (now LifePoint Church) was reaching 750 people in worship at the end of 1999, and by our second birthday in 2000, we were reaching 850 people each week. More than 2,450 people attended Easter 2000 services, and by May of 2000, CVC was averaging just under 1,000 people in attendance. Today, more than 1,600 people worship each weekend in a 700-seat auditorium on a thirty-nine-acre campus with 23,000 square feet under roof and more than 350 parking spaces on asphalt. In addition, the church helped to plant five churches in Reno and has launched two additional site campuses. We reach almost 2 percent of our surrounding population each weekend! Forty percent of the people who attend LifePoint Church each weekend were formerly unchurched. Many churches in the area have grown in their size and impact as well.

We feel that we've had a God-sized experience. But size alone was not the key. We were to later learn that all was not well in our midst.

The Emergence of LifePoint Church 2.0

From that point on, things went well at LifePoint Church, at least on the surface. But there were indications at the time that all was not well. For example, we had a nagging suspicion that our people were not growing toward greater maturity and clarity in their walks with God. However, we had no idea what a deeper examination of our reality would reveal. In the summer of 2004, many staff members were tired and overwhelmed. I had a clear sense that many of them were almost paralyzed, like deer in the headlights. The idea of reaching more people simply meant more work, and we were beginning to lose the passion that had once motivated us. Further, I was concerned that while our numbers were still strong, something was not right at the core. We continued to grow numerically until the spring of 2005, and then we hit what was to be our longest plateau and first decline. From the spring of 2005 until the fall of 2007, LifePoint Church lost members. Why did this happen, and could we have avoided it?

In hindsight, I think a variety of sociological factors were at work. In 2004 and early 2005, we were exceeding 80 percent of capacity in our worship center—many experts consider that to be the comfort level of most people in large-group settings—in both Sunday morning services, and although we still had room in our Saturday night services, people generally preferred to go at the "optimal inviting hour" on Sunday morning. Our key staff leaders were tired and frustrated as they confronted clear barriers such as overcrowding and logistics. We had only thirty minutes between services, yet it took twenty minutes to clear out the parking lot, and people were uncomfortably crowded in the hallways and children's classrooms.

Yet it wasn't merely these visible barriers that hindered us. Several of us were convinced that other factors were at work. The more we evaluated our circumstances, the more we began to believe that we had inadvertently catered to and created a consumerist culture. People chose to participate in an ever-increasing amount of church-sponsored events and programs, but much of that activity did not directly contribute to spiritual growth. Further, the more we examined the six-year history of the church, the more we felt that we were not systemically creating disciples. Yes, there were real and glorious stories of life change. But from a systemic standpoint (see chapter 7 for additional details), we were failing to fulfill our mission of seeing unchurched people become disciples of Jesus Christ.

The Emergence of LifePoint Church 3.0

From 2004 to 2007, seven major staff people left. Six departures had to do with leadership, philosophy of ministry, or demographic issues in our area. The seventh staff member left because of a moral failure. Many among our church family, and particularly our staff and governing board, found this period very painful. For a great part of this time, I was reading John 15. There Jesus tells us that a branch that doesn't bear fruit will be cut off and that a branch that does bear fruit will be pruned to bear more fruit. In John 15, Jesus tells his disciples that he has chosen them to bear fruit—fruit that remains. My clear sense was that we were not consistently bearing that kind of fruit in our first few years of ministry.

Now that I have been away from LifePoint Church for a period of time (I concluded my active ministry there in early 2010), I have continued to reflect on the the realities of what it means to be a God-sized ministry in a community. Developing disciples is a process, not a product, so we all must continue to ask God for wisdom and direction in our ministries. In hindsight, I am convinced that many of the struggles we were having in the ministry were a result of poor leadership on my part. Other factors included our lack of ability to attract and develop key high-level leaders quickly enough for the size and complexity of the church. As I have spent time thinking through our struggles, I have had to come to grips with my portion of the leadership gaps and trust God's grace and mercy for what was left undone.

Part of my reason for sharing what is in this chapter is to reveal to you the source of my passion. My passion comes from my vision and from my pain. We saw God at work among us in huge ways, and we made some really bad mistakes. But each step of the way, we sensed that God wanted a God-sized church in our community. The more I talk with people around the country, I know that God wants your church to move beyond numbers and to believe him for life changes that bear fruit for his glory in the years to come.

What motivates all of this? At the God-sized church I was privileged to lead, we had a fundamental commitment to the authority of God's Word and the central priority of the Great Commission. We said that we're all about "friends helping friends follow Christ." That has become more than a slogan at CVC. We've tried to embed it into our DNA. The journey of these years was torturous in many respects. (More about that later!) However, we have been encouraged by hundreds of other churches and leaders who are watching God do his work in their lives and ministries. We are deeply passionate about helping churches and leaders experience the God-sizing of their churches!

chapter 4

GOD-SIZE YOUR VISION

Good managers organize for efficiency. Good leaders direct for effectiveness. Great leaders galvanize and mobilize for breakthrough. Great leaders take their teams to greater heights than previously thought possible. So, what does a great leader in a God-sized church do? I think great leaders have four jobs.

1. *Casting a vision.* Great leaders cast a vision of the future that is preferable to the present. Casting a vision is all about seeing the future with a God's-eye view and painting the picture in compelling ways that cause people to risk the security of today for the hope of tomorrow.

2. *Creating environments.* Great leaders establish a greenhouse for their teams where mission, vision, and values can flourish. Creating the right environment allows greatness to prosper; the wrong environment kills creativity and destroys dreams.

3. *Developing systems.* Great leaders don't just do pie-in-the-sky thinking. Great leaders deal with on-the-ground realities, and they create systems for relationships, process, and support mechanisms to further the life and vision of their organizations.

4. *Equipping other leaders.* Great leaders always multiply value in the lives of others by giving away leadership to others. Great leaders are not threatened by other leaders but instead are energized by them. Equipping others means the whole team grows toward the future.

The following chapters provide more details for each of the four roles as you endeavor to God-size your church. This chapter begins with casting a vision. You are in a position to influence change in your church. Your mastery of these four roles will equip you for effective ministry leadership.

How does a local church God-size its vision? Several years ago, I developed a graphic that illustrates this three-step process: we are gripped by God's call, we grasp the needs of our community, and we recognize the gifts within our church family. This cycle begins when we are first gripped by the vision, but it is often repeated over time in the development of the ministry.

God's vision for your ministry must grip your soul before it can grab the heart of anyone else. Vision casting begins when the heart of God touches your heart. Only as you grapple with what he wants in your life will you be able to move into the new and challenging dimensions of ministry that he has for you and for your church. A church's vision must be clear if the church desires to reach and change people in the community, and a church's vision

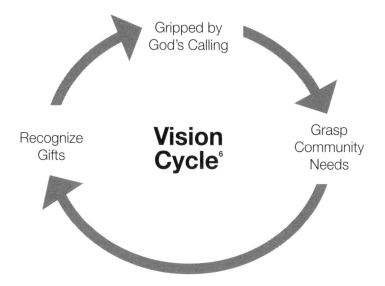

begins in the heart of its leaders. If the vision does not involve outreach, the church will face a significant growth barrier.

Once you have been *gripped* by God's vision for you and for your ministry, you can start to *grasp* the needs of the community. *God-sized churches long to reach people for Jesus Christ.* If your vision is to care for the contented, then you will not produce passion in your people to reach those outside the boundaries of the church family. Walt Kallestad's book *Turn Your Church Inside Out* is an accessible, compelling reference for helping you and your church make clear its vision to reach unchurched people. Every church that wants to be God-sized will look for tangible ways to be Jesus in its local community in order to reach people and bring them to Christ. God-sized churches are both attractive and missional—they simultaneously attract people to them and go to where the people are to reach them. Sometimes in the current church leadership conversation it seems as though we have forgotten about the miracle of *and*. Church can and should be attractive *and* missional, reaching lost people for Christ on campus *and* in the community. God-sized vision leads churches to draw in the community and to take the good news of Jesus Christ out to the community as well.

Some call this "presence evangelism"—being present in the network of society, being present in the ministry to physical needs of people, and being present in the spiritual battle for people's souls. Gary McIntosh and Glen Martin write, "Churches that are effective reaching people for Christ see the needs of the unchurched, establish ministries that allow the church to be present in the community, and have a process by which they are able to draw these unchurched people into the safety of Christ and a local church."[7]

If you have been *gripped* by God's vision for you and your church, if you have then *grasped* the specific needs of your community through which you can reach people in the name of Christ, you must then understand the *gifts* that God has entrusted to you and to your leadership core. Developing a committed group of core leaders who share your vision, who have passion for the community, and who recognize their God-given gifts is key to the health of a God-sized church. In fact, the core leadership of a healthy church must be unified in vision, in harmony with one another, and committed to community-focused ministry. Larry Osborne's book *The Unity Factor* makes the point that churches that push forward with programs, activities, and structure without unity do so at their peril. Countless stories of church division and difficulty can be told about churches that never arrived at unity of purpose and vision. A growing church that remains healthy in the long term will be led by a leader who understands the imperative of developing unity and cohesiveness among key leaders.

Recognizing your God-given gifts will equip your leadership team to develop specific plans for ministry. In almost all circumstances, you will need to focus on foundational core ministries like worship services, small groups, and children's and youth ministries. As you trust God, he will show you the key leadership people for these core ministry roles. In addition, however, he will link your vision and passion for ministry with your understanding of the key needs in your community, giving your ministry a distinctive appeal in your community. For instance, LifePoint Church recognized the importance of the performing arts in its community. We regularly prayed and tried to make space for artists and the performing arts to grow in our church. Each year we would provide one or more opportunities to share a glorious offering of the arts to our community that we believed would reach many for Christ. That would not happen if we had not recognized and made space for the gifts that we believe God wanted to lift up among us.

God-sizing your vision is critical to God-sizing your church. It isn't about being large, but it is about being filled with passion. If you are passionate about God's call and are gripped by it, if you are sensitive to and grasp the needs of your community, and if you recognize and call forth the gifts of your leadership team, God will grow your church. When churches have God-sized vision, what they want for their communities matches what God wants for their communities, and he is pleased to bless them and work through them. God loves it when your leadership influences your community in such a way that he receives honor.

What God longs to do in and through you begins in his own heart, and it is there that you must begin as well. Go hear from him, and then lead your people into the center of his heartbeat for your church and community!

chapter 5

GOD-SIZE YOUR CHURCH ENVIRONMENTS

An effective leader understands the importance of creating God-sized environments. The right sort of environment creates passion, allows creativity to flow, and raises people to their best potential selves—while the wrong sort of environment can stifle passion and growth.

Four key factors in creating God-sized environments affect your ability to reach your community: (1) understanding the community you seek to reach; (2) creating weekend worship environments that connect with the community; (3) developing special events that appeal to the community and provide special invite-and-serve opportunities for your people; and (4) designing spaces in which people can connect in relationships to one another and spiritual growth is encouraged. Let's take a closer look at each of these four factors in order to gain a deeper understanding of what a God-sized environment is and why it is so important.

(1) *Understanding the community you seek to reach.* God-sized church leaders are effective students of the culture of their community. It is helpful to review basic information about the makeup of your community, [8] and it is always vital to pray that God will give you spiritually discerning eyes to understand the reality of your area. When you are God-sizing your church, look at the context and conduct of your ministry. Of greatest importance is understanding the living, breathing nature of your community. You must learn to exegete your culture as you do the Scriptures, since you are engaged in a missionary task as a leader of a God-sized church. What are the factors that influence and motivate the people who live in your area? What are the everyday personal, family, economic, social, and spiritual pressures of people in your community? God-sized ministry always finds ways to connect with the community and meets needs in the name of Jesus. Are you a student of the community where God has called you, and do you know how God has specifically called you to create environments to meet those particular needs?

(2) *Creating weekend worship environments that connect with the community.* Ed Young of Fellowship Church in Dallas (www.fellowshipchurch.com), in his monthly leadership CD series titled *Leadership Uncensored,* says, "It is all about the weekend, stupid." At our church in northern Nevada, we modified Ed's saying a little: "It all starts with the weekend." Churches that God-size their ministries will be acutely aware of how their weekend services connect with people and help them move toward Christ and spiritual health. God-sizing your ministry means understanding the community and ensuring that the weekend services connect the timeless truths of God's Word to the daily reality of people's lives. Further, helping people experience and

encounter God in an environment of worship and biblical community is central to a vibrant church life.

We took some principles of *The Purpose Driven Church* by Rick Warren and developed a model to visualize what it looks like to move people through a variety of environments toward spiritual health and maturity. Here is our diagram as it existed at LifePoint Church:

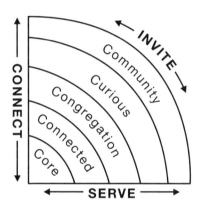

The community is the place where God has called us to serve. One friend of mine says he is serving a church of eight thousand (the size of his community), but only four hundred attend his church! The curious are those who have at least "tasted or sampled" the ministry of your church. The congregation consists of those who are in fairly regular contact with you, though not really relationally connected. The connected consists of those who are relationally engaged where someone knows their name and they are loved and prayed for. The core of the church is those who are connected in relationships and have a meaningful place to serve.

Each of our designations in the diagram (Community, Curious, Congregation, Connected, Core) relates to environments we have designed to help people move from the weekend services into deeper relationships and the fulfillment of God's plan for their lives. Have you designed your weekend worship services in such a way that you are helping people connect to God, his Word, and his plan for their lives?

(3) *Developing special events that appeal to the community and provide special invite-and-serve opportunities for your people.* Hosting or participating in significant events provides a tool for reaching a broad spectrum of your local community. In each community, there is a natural rhythm to the year, and there are likely natural events that your church can connect with or partner with in order to reach the greatest number of people for Christ. Our church in Nevada used the Fourth of July as a special event. Bayside Church provides a "Trunk or Treat" Halloween event and a host of local outreach experiences during the holiday seasons of November and December to mobilize people to connect with the community. Over time I have become convinced that these events provide a special link for our people both to invite and to serve the community. Inviting someone to a special event rather than a weekend worship service is often an easier first step. Do you have any specially designed outreach events that help your people to reach, to invite, and to serve your community?

(4) *Designing spaces in which people can connect in relationships to one another and spiritual growth is encouraged.* When a ministry begins to influence the culture, the community, and the crowd at the weekend services, God-sizing leaders develop environments where people can be in biblical community with one another. One study of effective churches concluded, "Effective

churches have specific ministries designed to help people break down the walls of confrontation, isolation, stagnation, and fragmentation. These ministries make the people accountable to one another and urge the people to continue to move forward in their growth."[9] Are there groups, classes, teams, and contexts at your church in which people can grow in their relationships with God and with one another? Such growth is a fundamental part of a Christian's spiritual journey, and we cannot have God-sized churches if we aren't creating environments that encourage people to grow in love for each other and God.

God-sized churches are creative design centers. Even as they call the people to worship, to repentance, to discipleship, to ministry, and to holiness, God-sized churches are determined to constantly move creatively toward life and health. Leaders of God-sized churches are equally passionate for evangelism and discipleship, and they recognize the imperative of creating environments that accomplish these purposes. Like a greenhouse that allows plants to grow, flourish, and bear fruit in all seasons, a church that creates God-sized environments can impact its community year after year.

chapter 6

GOD-SIZE YOUR SYSTEMS

The third task of an effective God-sizing leader is the development of systems that support the vision, mission, and values of the organization. Alvin Toffler says, "You've got to think about big things while you're doing small things, so that all the small things go in the right direction." [10] If a church is going to be God-sized *later*, it is imperative that its leaders think about the church's systems *now*. A. A. Milne, creator of the beloved Winnie-the-Pooh books, puts a perfect definition of *organization* in the mouth of Christopher Robin: "Organizing is what you do before you do something, so that when you do it, it's not all mixed up." [11]

In my former context in Nevada, we had a vision for spiritual transformation. Our slogan was "Friends helping friends follow Christ." We created three primary systems to support that vision: inviting systems, which provide an opportunity to reach people for Christ; connecting systems, which engage people in authentic relationships for spiritual health; and serving systems, in which people discover their spiritual gifts and develop their leadership skills. I have seen churches of all sizes recognize the need to develop specific systems to reach people, care for them, and equip them for ministry.

Large organizations can quickly take on a character of their own—a character that may not match the intentions of their founders. In *The Very Large Church*, Lyle Schaller explains that social environments have become much more complex, anonymous, and hostile. Since larger institutions are increasingly part of the fabric of our society, larger churches are as well. One of the realities of larger organizations is that they are complex; similar to the human body, they are a set of interrelated systems. God-sizing leaders will develop systems to accomplish the vision that God has given them for their organizations, *before the organizations become too big to guide*.

The human body provides a useful way of thinking about the systems of a church family. God designed the body with several major systems—such as the circulatory, digestive, and immune systems—that all work together. God is the master system designer, whether in the human body or in the church, the body of Christ. Each system in the body serves a necessary and specific purpose, is interrelated with the other systems, and is essential for health. The church also has a number of specific ministry systems essential for a church to become a thriving, God-sized community of faith:

- an *evangelistic* system to help your people reach other people for Christ
- an *assimilation* system to help connect new people to the life of the church family
- a *discipleship* system to help grow people from spiritual infancy to spiritual maturity

- a *healing* system to help people become free from the bondage of pain in their lives
- a *ministry* system to help people discover and use their gifts to serve others for the glory of God
- a *mission* system to help mobilize Christ followers to serve their communities and the world

It is beyond the scope of this book to fully detail each system, but I will explain a bit about how each of them functions in a God-sized church. I also make the specific assumption that a truly biblical church is deeply committed to the corporate experience of gathering together for worship. The people of God gather for worship to connect our hearts to God, for teaching to connect our minds to God, and for ministry to equip us for living out our faith in everyday life. A church that is faithful in worship and gathering together establishes the foundation for God-sizing the ministry through the various systems of a healthy church family.

Evangelistic System

A church with a healthy evangelistic system consistently feels the heartbeat of Christ for the lost in its community, and it acts on that feeling with specific programs of outreach. There are any number of ways for a church to cultivate an evangelistic heart, but most effective evangelistic systems are built on the pillars of relational evangelism, invitational evangelism, and missional evangelism. In relational evangelism, church leaders equip people to share their faith naturally and comfortably with persons they know who have not been introduced to Christ.

Invitational evangelism equips people to invite their friends and circle of influence to services, activities, and events at the church so that they can then come to know Christ. Missional evangelism is about being the hands and heart of Jesus in the local community by responding to the direct needs of people with acts of compassion, justice, mercy, and kindness. A God-sized church will consistently monitor its evangelistic temperature to ensure that it burns as hot as the heart of God.

Assimilation System

God-sized churches have a passion to connect disconnected people with each other and with God, a mission that is often accomplished in the faith community through small groups. A fully functioning assimilation system typically offers introductory classes, follow-up mechanisms, and ways to integrate people into small groups or classes at the earliest possible time. For many people, the easiest door out of the church is the huge back door because they have never been properly connected to other believers by well-designed assimilation systems. God-sizing leaders looking for the best reference work on assimilation should check out *Fusion: Integrating Newcomers into the Life of Your Church* by Nelson Searcy and Jennifer Henson. Leading a God-sized church means developing a proper assimilation system to ensure that people get connected, stay connected, and welcome others into the family of God.

Discipleship System

Attracting unchurched people to Sunday-morning worship is not the primary aim of a God-sized church. The primary focus of every biblical church is to fulfill the Great Commission in Matthew 28:19–20, which commands us to go *into* the world and make disciples. Willow Creek Community Church in Chicago (www.willowcreek.org) has for years professed its mission "to turn irreligious people into fully devoted followers of Christ." The mission statement of LifePoint Church is to see "unchurched people become disciples of Jesus Christ," and its vision statement is about the "spiritual transformation of Northern Nevada and the Mountain West." A healthy God-sized church is focused on making disciples; reaching people is the *beginning*, not the *end* of a God-sized church.

God-sizing your church will require the development of a discipleship system. In this context, a discipleship system that is working well can bring someone from spiritual infancy to spiritual maturity through a process of study, relationships, mentoring, and mastery of truths and practices central to the faith. A recent study, REVEAL (www.revealnow.com), unveils several of the most effective discipleship steps that churches are using today. Fundamentally, a discipleship system will help people understand God's Word and apply it in their lives for spiritual growth and maturity while in relationship with the community of faith. That, in turn, will send healthy disciples back out into the community to reach and attract more disciples.

Healing System

People are messy. We are broken at the core and in need of a Savior and a Healer. Jesus Christ longs for us to be free from the pain of our past and the imperfect reality of our present, and to give us hope for the future (Jeremiah 29:11). A God-sized church provides a variety of care systems to ensure that people can be loved, encouraged, and challenged and receive healing from the hand of God. Most of these healing systems are within the connecting environments of the church, where specific ministry can happen within small groups or very personalized settings.

Ministry System

The Bible teaches very clearly that every Christian has at least one spiritual gift (1 Corinthians 12:4–11) and that God has placed us strategically within his family so that we can contribute to the proper working of the whole by doing our individual part (Ephesians 4:1–16). Discovering our spiritual gifts is an important part of being an effective God-sized church, since it is only then that we can understand the unique calling God has for us. If a willing Christian is forced to teach Sunday school for ten years, even when her gifts are in the field of fund-raising, she is being set up for burnout, and the church is being hindered from becoming God-sized. Wise leaders ensure that their ministry systems aren't about filling in gaps in an organizational chart, but rather about equipping each member to discover and use his or her unique, God-given gifts. (More on this in the next chapter.) Two excellent resources that address this issue are *The*

Purpose-Driven Church by Rick Warren and *Doing Church as a Team* by Wayne Cordeiro.

Mission System

For far too long, churches have often invited people to "come and see us." Today, many God-sized churches recognize the need to be Jesus with skin on in their local communities and around the world. Matthew 5:13–16 exhorts us to be salt and light and live our lives in such a way that people see our good works and glorify our Father in heaven. Ephesians 2:10 tells us that God actually prepared good works for us before the foundation of the world. A God-sized church views the needs in the community as opportunities to touch hurting and wounded people with the love and kindness of Jesus. When the life of Jesus gets lived out locally and globally, the church will become more like Christ, and the communities will be drawn to him. Leadership Network has been helping create a movement of Externally Focused Churches; for more information, see its website at www.externallyfocusednetwork.com.

The church is the body of Christ, an intricate and interconnected system designed by God for his glory and for the salvation and transformation of the world. Each system referenced above is a key piece in an integrated whole. Remove one of the systems, and the church family will not grow in a healthy and God-honoring way. In my experience, when churches fail to properly conceive or execute one of these essential church systems, those churches miss the mark in tangible ways. God-sized churches are organizations that function in concert, with each system part of a glorious whole. These effective, interlocking systems don't happen by accident but are the product of prayerful vision, careful, strategic planning, and consistent execution. God-sizing leaders think about effective systems when the organization is small, providing the trajectory for that organization to grow toward God's glory.

For this to happen, a church must be led by the right kinds of leaders. The next chapter will help us God-size our leadership-equipping systems so that we can develop healthy disciples of Jesus Christ and God-size our churches.

chapter 7

GOD-SIZE YOUR LEADERS

A thletes and entertainers structure their lives for peak performance, but the body of Christ often functions in a very different way. Athletes eat properly, exercise religiously, and tone their bodies so they are at their optimum efficiency on the day of the event. In the same way, entertainers practice for hours and prepare with others in the band, symphony, or group so they are at their best when the lights come on and the crowd cheers. Whether the rewards are tangible (financial or public acclaim) or intangible (pride of accomplishment), peak performers aim for success and structure their lives and efforts to achieve optimal output.

In the church, however, instead of preparing people for peak performance, we often use people to fill positions in an organizational chart we have developed. When we need a second-grade teacher for Sunday school, we find somebody—anybody!—who will say yes, even if we have to use guilt to motivate our members. We need a different value system. We need to help people find the place where they can fulfill their calling, serve in their area of giftedness, and see God use them in their sweet spot. We need to inspire people to excellence instead of using them to fill empty slots.

God-sizing leaders cast visions, create environments, develop systems, and equip leaders. This final step in the cycle ensures that the vision and mission of the church will be passed forward and developed, instead of fizzling out after a few years. Most church leaders recognize the importance of equipping leaders but are vexed by the actual experience of doing it. In this chapter, I want to explore four specific practices that will help you equip leaders on the way to God-sizing your church: life-on-life, skill training, benchmarking, and leadership development.

Life-on-Life

Equipping leaders is, at its core, about relationships. It takes time and energy to speak into the lives of others and grow and develop them as leaders. The best way I know to plant hope and truth into a person's heart is to do life together. Relational shaping involves spending formal and informal time together, much like the development of any healthy relationship. The process of equipping leaders reminds me of a combination of dating, marriage, parenting, and team sports! By the way, *every* time I've had a leadership failure on my teams, a significant factor has been that we didn't stay connected life-on-life. This, of course, raises the issue of how many people you can equip at one time. The answer varies, but if you are talking about intensive equipping, the number is fewer than you think. (This is especially true if you are a Commander-style leader; see my book *Leveraging Your*

Leadership Style to explore that subject.) However, we can agree that equipping a few effective leaders is far superior to "equipping" a high number of leaders who have no idea what they're doing!

To facilitate life-on-life equipping, make sure that various teams in your church do things like hang out for coffee with no formal agenda, spend time in each other's homes, and have recreational fun together. You'll certainly spend intensive time with each other in ministry-specific settings, like meeting, services, and formal events, so casual events help flesh out the life-on-life relationship with different contexts and opportunities for friendship and growth. When you invest time in your team members by doing life together with intentionality, your ability to equip leaders and walk with them through the ups and downs of life will grow exponentially.

Skill Training

One meaning of the Hebrew word for training is "to make narrow." Skill training helps provide skills and strategic understandings for application in specific contexts. Often I have had the experience of a staff member describing a great program he has read about or seen someplace else. Those conversations then develop into great training moments where we can discuss the specifics of the context, the individual talents and skill sets required to produce the ministry result he is looking for, and the gaps in our existing knowledge.

Since vision is always more caught than taught, the process of training often provides great vision-refining moments. Given the abundance of training opportunities available to us in our modern American society, I think there really is no excuse for not sharpening the specific required skills for your team. A benefit of training together is that we learn better when we can recognize the differences in our various learning styles and appropriate what comes naturally to others. Effective training takes place when teams sharpen the skill sets of team members and increase both productivity and synergy by most effectively using the resources and talents of team members.

Benchmarking

At its worst, benchmarking is simply "monkey see, monkey do." If I see something good in another church, then I can ape it in my church. That is a terrible approach to equipping leaders because every ministry strategy must be adapted for your local setting and not simply adopted wholesale. At its best, however, benchmarking exposes your leadership team to greatness and sparks discussions about how your church might carry out ministry more effectively. Visiting other churches that are doing a noteworthy job in ministry can elevate the thinking of your leaders. Whenever I have the privilege of speaking to other teams, I strongly encourage them to develop the habit of visiting other God-sized churches in order to learn and be challenged. One practical idea is to provide funds for each member of your pastoral team to visit at least two other churches annually to learn their stories and benchmark their ministry practices. Another way to benchmark at a distance is to identify fifteen to twenty key church websites and visit them on a regular basis to see what is new and exciting. I encourage the leaders with whom I work to pay attention to churches that are at least double their size in order to learn how to scale up their systems to serve larger groups of people.

Benchmarking is about equipping leaders to be lifelong learners, because leaders who stop learning won't be leaders for long!

Leadership Development

We want to believe that leadership is about position and performance in a specific context, but leadership is a *process*, not an *event*. Equipping leaders to understand and experience the full measure of their leadership potential *over time* is an essential part of the leadership development process. All good leaders understand their responsibilities—their tasks, processes, organizational duties, etc.—but great leaders understand the importance of developing themselves, their people, and their shared vision over time. Truly effective leadership development results in long-term multiplication of leaders.

Consequently, because they want to keep growing in order to multiply their impact, God-sized churches see to it that people have shared experiences of working together, facing challenges, cultivating vision, and deepening their relationships with Christ and one another. Leadership equipping is not a solo sport! Effective leaders equip other leaders. That equipping ministry produces a ripple effect that reaches the shores of heaven. The apostle Paul was clear about that in 1 Thessalonians 2:19–20 when he wrote, "What is our hope, our joy, or the crown in which we will glory in the presence of our Lord Jesus when he comes? Is it not you? Indeed, you are our glory and joy." At our church, we say, "Changed lives are our business." We've learned over time that equipping leaders for long-term, consistent ministry is at the heart of our business!

Creating a steady stream of emerging leaders is a must for a God-sized church. Since all business is ultimately about people, we need to be willing to develop, care for, and cheer on the success of those who work with us, for us, and around us. Andrew Carnegie said his desired epitaph was, "Here lies a man who attracted better people into his service than he was himself." [12] Cultivating a life and a ministry that are inherently relational will improve your emotional health and will enhance the fruit of your labor as you lead your church to becoming a God-sized church.

chapter 8

LEADERSHIP BARRIERS TO GOD-SIZING YOUR CHURCH, PART 1

One day, Frank went fishing. As he established himself on one side of the lake, he noticed another man fishing on the other side. For the next three hours Frank had zero luck—he was getting skunked, as they say. What was even more frustrating was that he saw the guy on the other side of the lake catching and throwing back *big* fish on a regular basis! Frank finally marched over to the other side of the lake. "I've been watching you for three hours," said Frank. "Why in the world are you throwing back the largest fish you catch? I can't stand watching you do that!"

"It's simple," the stranger replied. Pulling a small frying pan out of his backpack, he said, "My frying pan is only this big."

Are you limited to your current ministry reality, or can you catch a God-sized dream? Are you willing and able to grow, or are there barriers in your vision, structure, or leadership that mean you'll always be stuck with the size and shape you are right now?

Churches and church leaders hit walls, get stuck, and settle for what seems normal. Often, barriers exist because of repeated patterns of behavior. Lyle Schaller calls this "path dependency." [13] Once people and/or institutions travel down a certain path, it is difficult to choose a new road. Having gotten what we have always gotten, we continue to do what we have always done. How many times have you been constrained by damaging or destructive patterns in your ministry? Barriers are part of the human condition, and any effective ministry must identify, confront, and overcome these barriers.

In this chapter and chapter 10, we'll look at six specific barriers to becoming God-sized that may be present in leadership, while in chapters 11, 12, and 13 we'll examine common barriers to growth. At the outset, then, it will be useful to differentiate between the two kinds of barriers. *A leadership barrier is a barrier that exists in the mind, the heart, or the gift mix of the church leader.* A growth barrier *is a set of qualitative factors that create a ceiling to quantitative progress.*

Starting with the core leadership of a church, then, let's examine the six primary barriers, the first three of which we'll dive into in this chapter. These are barriers of mind, heart, and teamwork:

1. The barrier of *vision*—a breakthrough of **clarity**
2. The barrier of *leadership*—a breakthrough of **certainty**
3. The barrier of *team*—a breakthrough of **unity**
4. The barrier of *community*—a breakthrough of **connection**

5. The barrier of *presentation*—a breakthrough of
   excellence

6. The barrier of *follow-through*—a breakthrough of
   faithfulness

I am indebted to Carl George and Warren Bird for introducing these categories in their excellent book *How to Break Growth Barriers.* [14] It is my goal, by examining each of these leadership barriers in light of the mission to God-size your church, to equip you in your leadership role, no matter what the current size of your organization. Then the following chapters will equip you regarding specific size barriers and how you can lead through them. The first three leadership barriers relate to your personal worldview and the relationships on your team, while the latter three, addressed in the next chapter, concern the way that your ministry conducts itself in your community.

Barrier #1: The Barrier of Vision:
A Breakthrough of Clarity

Cindi has been a committed volunteer at her church for the past five years. In fact, she tends to be a favorite around the church office with her uncompromising work ethic and ability to make things happen. Cindi is a model lay leader in many respects: hardworking, supportive of the church's mission and direction, and outreach oriented. She directs the early childhood education at the church, coordinates some outreach sports teams, and occasionally plays flute with the praise team.

After a challenging Christmas season, Cindi makes some changes to her priorities and scheduling to better balance family and ministry demands. No matter what she does, however, she cannot discover a creative solution to the problems that have been plaguing early childhood ministries for the last eight months. The elementary-age ministry is thriving and creating unique solutions to the issues it faces on a weekly basis, but in the early childhood classes, Cindi feels that she is banging her head against the wall. How should the department cope with issues like lack of space and increased attendance? No matter how hard she works, the solutions remain elusive. It's not that Cindi minds challenges, but a solution would be nice once in a while!

What Cindi needs is clarity, and her need is common to many church leaders. The reality of day-to-day ministry in the trenches—outreach, equipping, education, counsel, and crises—creates multiple demands for church leaders on a regular basis. If the church at large is unclear about its ultimate goals and objectives, individual programs and ministries cannot function in harmony with each other. This is a real problem, because if Cindi and her team don't find creative solutions to the problems plaguing their ministry, it will plateau and decline over time.

Cindi needs a clear vision for her subministry, a vision that is directly connected to the overarching vision of the church. Hard work gets things done, but it needs to be done in service to the vision. Cindi's ministry requires breaking through to clarity.

If it is true that everything rises and falls on the issue of leadership, it is also true that the leadership must have a clear vision of where it is going. If you don't know where you're going, you'll never know when you get there!

Vision starts with you. Many teenagers struggle with the question, "Why am I here?" But this wrestling match is not just reserved for teens! Many adults wrestle with this million-dollar question as well—finding our purpose on this earth is critical to our ability to find a "zone" of ministry and change lives forever. Clear vision starts with the question, "Why did God create me and put me in this place at this time?" As you search and find that answer, you will also find more clarity in how your own leadership impacts the vision of your church or ministry organization.

Clarity of vision must answer the questions, "For whom does my church exist? And how will we serve them?"

Leaders of God-sized churches know who they are, why they are, and where they are. They have learned to operate out of their strengths and to mitigate their weaknesses. They know their key role and how to parlay that role into motivated ministry. Leaders of God-sized churches know where they are going, and they help their communities of faith get there. They have a vision, and they help their team see that vision with clarity and then accomplish it—which is exactly what workers like Cindi need.

Barrier #2: The Barrier of Leadership: A Breakthrough of Certainty

Pastor Jerry looked around the conference room at the members of his staff—all five of them. The associate pastor of the last two years was performing above average and led the community care ministries. The youth pastor often looked tired, but things were going fine with the youth, and there hadn't been any complaints about the rough-and-tough new high schoolers in ten months, a new church record. The secretary/communications director was doing her work duties well enough, but she didn't support Jerry's leadership the way he hoped a key staffer would, and she was divisive in the office. The outreach director (still a volunteer position) was doing his job acceptably, but he had worked for a lengthier time under the previous senior pastor and continued to espouse the former leader's position on various issues. The worship leader continued to butt heads with Jerry—not about the type of music, but about the length of the worship set within the service.

The church was poised to have a huge positive impact on the community of 180,000. The church had a prime location—when the fifteen acres next door were donated to the church, the transaction made the front page of the city paper. They had a great buzz in the community and almost limitless potential. Yet as Jerry looked around the room, he realized that in the midst of all the potential, he had a mediocre team.

When he left the meeting, he decided to do something about it.

Hoping for a quick fix, Jerry called Don, a mentor three hours away, to ask—gasp!—for help! *He won't have time to help me,* Jerry thought as he dialed the number. *He's probably not even receiving calls today.* But in a serendipitous moment, the secretary patched him directly through, and Don sounded happy to hear his voice. As luck would have it (read: God), Don was to be in the area in two weeks, and they arranged to have a long lunch while they discussed strategy. The outcome was dramatic:

- The associate was gifted, but almost all of the gifts were in Jerry's areas of expertise. The care groups were hobbling along, but the associate's passions were in the areas of teaching and exposition—and he had the gift of leadership like Jerry did. The solution: put his leadership and teaching gifts to good use in a young adult/young family outreach-style ministry outside of Sunday morning. It took off like a rocket, and the associate essentially served as pastor of that subcongregation, which thrived under his leadership.

- The outreach pastor had some good ideas, but he was stuck in the past. Jerry had lunch with him and explained some strains in the team related to the outreach position. The staffer accepted the pastor's critique and formed an outreach team that included lay leaders. They took on visitor follow-up with passion and excellence.

- Jerry discussed the worship possibilities with Don and came up with creative solutions to the children's ministry problems that were preventing the adults from adding ten minutes to their service. Doing that eased the worship leader's frustration and gave the whole congregation what it really wanted in the first place—more time to worship.

- There was some flexibility with staffing since the children's director had recently moved and the position was vacant. For some time, Jerry wanted to move a key lay leader into a staff position, but the communications director in the office was tying up resources that could have been better used. He met with the communications director, discussed the staffing changes, and gave her two months to find another job. She found another job in five days and quit early. This change allowed Jerry to bring the key lay leader onto the staff into the children's director role and make the communications role a lay-led position.

- Jerry brought in training resources for the youth staffer to help him build a stronger team of volunteers so that less of the work fell on his shoulders.

This is but one example that happened to work because of the flexibility of the senior leader and the other members of the team. I realize they don't all go this direction. I've had my share of team failures over the years, but I want you to have hope. It can work!

Pastoral leaders with a clear vision understand the importance of aligning people's gifts and passions with the purposes of the church. Developing a winning team means the senior leader surrounds himself or herself with people who have complementary gifts, share the vision of the ministry, and are willing to work in a team environment.

All the time Pastor Jerry thought the problem was with other elements of the ministry, it was actually with his own leadership! He lacked the certainty to make difficult but necessary changes to the church staff and structure. Bold, confident leadership was required, and when Jerry stepped up to that task, the solutions became clear.

Ministry is war, as Paul reminds us. You are on the battlefield with a team of people who will either gain ground, lose ground, or huddle in a foxhole. The barrier of leadership can seem insurmountable, but the success of your ministry depends on your willingness to boldly take responsibility for the mission. Your team can advance only when the members know their roles with certainty.

Barrier #3: The Barrier of Team:
A Breakthrough of Unity

Doug and Lisa fell in love at first sight—almost. Doug had been interested in Lisa ever since they met at the college group's all-night party at the nearby amusement park. But since Doug accidentally spilled his hot coffee all over Lisa's back while they were in line for the big roller coaster, it took a few weeks for Lisa to become interested in Doug.

Doug was a gifted teacher in the adult small-group ministry at the church. He wasn't called by God into vocational ministry, but he recognized his gifts and enjoyed using them in ministry. Lisa (after recovering from the coffee incident) also became committed to ministry at the church. Although she had spent a few years bouncing from ministry area to ministry area, she ultimately caught a vision for the fifth- and sixth-grade department and went wild there. It was a perfect fit: the kids loved her energy, her passion for God, and her relevance; and she loved helping to shape the kids' values before they faced the pressures of middle school. During their engagement and subsequent marriage, Doug and Lisa led the young adult small group at the church, and Lisa team-taught the fifth- and sixth-grade Sunday school class.

Pastor Jim loved Doug and Lisa. He hadn't personally led them to Christ, but from the day he started at the church, he knew that they were a dynamic, influential couple who were, in his words, "keepers." Not only was their love for God evident in what they did, but their commitment to invest in the lives of others shone through their weekly ministry projects. They were a delight to have at the church, and every year they seemed to be more and more effective.

About six years after their wedding, which Jim performed, he asked Doug out to lunch and challenged him to serve on the church leadership team. Their church had a one-board leadership structure, and being asked to serve was a privilege usually given to people in their thirties and older. Jim didn't want Doug's age (twenty-eight) to be a barrier for him, and Doug said yes. The other board members were pleased with Doug's and Lisa's track records and heartily welcomed him to the board. His nomination and vote were unchallenged.

It wasn't long, though, before Doug started dreading the meetings. They were not openly contentious by any means, and no one received a black eye. But there was something he couldn't put his finger on—something that distressed him. He served three years on the board and continued to teach Bible studies, while Lisa took over the fifth- and sixth-grade ministry. Soon forty preteens were coming to their midweek ministry night!

The more Doug worked alongside other leaders in problem solving, the more he realized that a particular group at the church didn't support Jim's pastorate. It wasn't that they disliked him personally (although a few did); they simply didn't support the vision. The tension ate at Doug's stomach every time the board met.

Over lunch one afternoon, Doug and Pastor Jim openly discussed the issue. It turned out that things were worse than Doug knew. A faction on the board had asked Jim to resign, and an entire adult Sunday school class had written him a letter to that effect. They knew "what they wanted in a church," and they knew Jim "was not the man to lead it." Jim had been looking for other work, but he didn't feel released from his ministry assignment yet, so he was persevering despite the opposition.

The situation worsened. Members of the contentious group started calling Doug at work and at home. Doug couldn't discern whether the things he was hearing were true, false, or a little of both. Lisa's heart was getting heavier, and her ministry with the preteens was suffering. Furthermore, Lisa's students were picking up information from different sources, and that caused them to ask questions about churches and pastors that she was simply unprepared to answer. Life was hard, and it wasn't getting easier. Doug internalized much of his anger and hopelessness and ultimately developed an ulcer.

The strain of ministry conflict was getting worse, and Doug's health was not good. When his doctor asked him if he needed a medical leave from his job, Doug realized that what he really needed was a medical leave from his church. In the midst of a strained and difficult ministry environment at a church Doug and Lisa loved, they began the heart-rending decision process of whether to leave.

Over time it became clear that they couldn't continue to minister effectively in a church where ugliness and meanness increasingly won out over love and reconciliation. After twelve months of soul-searching and many nights of tears, Doug and Lisa left the church. They had never felt less unified with a local church in their lives.

The hard truth is this: *without leadership unity, there will be no lasting ministry growth that breaks through barriers.* My friend Don Nelson is a committed lay leader in a church that has worked with several church plants to help them launch well. He sent me a note in 2001 describing the divisiveness in his church:

At our church, my wife and I are giving time we don't have, and tons of money because it's important. Do you think we are going to let sick people kill that work and investment? Heavens no! It's costing us way too much! For every sick, agenda-laden, divisive, contentious person in our church we aren't willing to confront (out of fear, we say, "Oh, that's just the way they are," or "I don't think God wants us to treat people like that," etc.), there are ten, twenty, one hundred, one thousand people out there to be won to Christ who won't because they sniff out the contentiousness and will go somewhere else. Do we want to stand before God and say we did the math wrong, or that we didn't have the guts to make way for hundreds more to come to Christ by not tackling these problems decisively? [15]

We cannot let the impact of our churches be limited by divided leadership. Unified leadership is the only way to ensure that a church has the unity and vision to punch through barriers to growth. No current hardship related to confronting division can be worse for the church than long-term division.

In a God-sized church, community life in the church family is so honored that division and gossip are confronted quickly and clearly and resolved in accordance with biblical principles of fellowship and conflict resolution. Matthew 18:15–17 discusses specifically what we are to do if a believer sins against us and how we are to go about reconciliation. It is critically important that we face conflict and its related issues head-on so that the mess of unresolved issues does not fester and seethe:

If your brother or sister sins, go and point out their fault, just between the two of you. If they listen to you, you have won them over. But if they will not listen, take one or two others along, so that "every matter may be established by the testimony of two or three witnesses." If they still refuse to listen to them, tell it to the church; and if they refuse to listen even to the church, treat them as you would a pagan or a tax collector.

A God-sized church must have its core leadership unified in the vision, in relationship with one another, and committed together in ministry to the community. Countless stories of church division and difficulty can be told about churches that never arrived at unity of purpose and vision. A growing church will be led by a leader who understands the imperative of developing unity and cohesiveness among the key leaders and who has the courage to confront division and make changes when necessary.

A God-sized church is always clear about the call to maturity. When believers are constantly bickering, creating a climate of backbiting and division, the potential for effective kingdom ministry is virtually nonexistent. Leaders must model and exhort their congregations toward spiritual maturity and present visible patterns of conflict resolution that engender authentic community within the family. Tragically, many churches have chosen the path of least resistance, rather than the avenue of greatest spiritual impact. Parents know that failing to confront their children leads to long-term difficulties, but church leaders are often tempted to maintain an appearance of acceptance and non-confrontation.

GOD-SIZE YOUR CHURCH

Unity must be present to break through growth barriers. Some churches are so conflicted and contentious that a long-term solution is far from reach. But in many cases, the church has simply failed to teach and practice the Matthew 18 principles of conflict resolution and the sin-forgiveness process. What could happen in the kingdom of God if more churches decided to face sin and conflict in a godly manner?

These first three leadership barriers—the barriers of vision, leadership, and team—are barriers of heart, mind, and team-work. Any one of them can prevent your church from having the influence and impact that God desires. Every leadership barrier has unique contours and contexts, but these large patterns are distressingly common. Godly leaders must be willing to confront these barriers, leading their churches and communities into clarity, certainty, and unity—and closer to the kingdom of God.

chapter 9

LEADERSHIP BARRIERS TO GOD-SIZING YOUR CHURCH, PART 2

I n the previous chapter, we reviewed three leadership barriers that relate primarily to the worldview of the leader and the team around that leader. In this chapter, the next three leadership barriers relate to the context of the community in which you serve. Former Senator Tip O'Neill wrote *All Politics Is Local* in 1994 to describe the reality that all politics comes down to personal impact. Likewise, all ministry is local. Grand plans, strategies, and dreams ultimately relate to the power of God to change a human heart. Until we see transformation in human life, we have not succeeded in experiencing what a God-sized ministry is all about. These next three barriers will help us understand that in clear detail.

Barrier #4: The Barrier of Community:
A Breakthrough of Connection

Pastor Dave sat at the deacons meeting, listening to the latest report from the food pantry coordinator, but his mind was somewhere else. He was daydreaming about what the church was like five years earlier. Then the church was bursting at the seams. Momentum was on their side. Young families were joining the church at record speed, and mature adults were reaching out to the community in strategic ways. Dave remembered reporting one year that the two hundred people who joined the church in the previous two years equally represented all the age brackets! Their church was truly intergenerational, and everyone loved it.

The mission team did a study of the church's local community of 600,000 and learned about strategic needs that county social services had identified but not yet funded. New need-based ministries were started and thrived. Young families learned the importance of a Christ-centered marriage and family, and children were taught the gospel from an early age. The church was buzzing with activity, and you could feel the energy on a Sunday morning when you walked around.

Pastor Dave snapped out of his daydream and wondered what had gone wrong. In actuality, nothing had gone wrong. The church was just as poised for influence as it had been, *but it was poised to influence a different community.* The surrounding community had changed right under their noses in only five years, and the church hadn't taken notice. Both of the air force bases within thirty-five miles had closed, and only a small percentage of the work force remained behind as the bases transitioned to civilian industries. A brand-new retirement village was built in a small community forty-five miles south of the church. Positioned on three golf courses, this residential behemoth (with houses, apartments, partial-care and total-care facilities) was attracting a huge number of mature adults from the surrounding communities. Many young families liked the school district in that southern suburb and were moving there, and six months previously that community incorporated and became its own municipality.

Pastor Dave could list nearly two hundred people who had left his church because of these demographic shifts. Their steady stream of visitors was still showing up each Sunday, but the visitors themselves were different. The city was not dwindling—the population had actually gown substantially in the last year, and the church could have a dramatic impact if it understood the new community that had developed around it. How would the church thrive and grow in the next five years? Longing for the past wouldn't solve anything, but what else could the church members and leaders do?

God-sized churches *always* know their communities, and knowing a community means studying it. Who lives near your church? Where do they work? How long have they lived there, and where do their kids go to school? What ministry needs are present in particular neighborhoods? Imagine your ministry is located in a community where the average annual household income is $80,000. How would your outreach focus be different from that of a church located in the center of a college community with thousands of single people? The heart of the gospel will never change, but the way we advertise, perform music, speak, and minister can be vastly different. If the local McDonald's owner knows more about your community and how to reach it than you do as a pastor, your church is in trouble. Barrier-busting ministry always finds a way to connect with the community and meet needs in the name of Christ.

A friend of mine pastors a church in a changing area. Previously, the work force commuted to towns up to an hour away. That meant workers got home late at night and had difficulty participating in midweek activities. Now, the work force has shifted, and people work closer to home. While people can now work in the same town where they live and worship, the community is faster paced, more heterogeneous, and sometimes dangerous. As their sleepy little town becomes a bustling city, my friend's church now offers a menu of parent and family activities centered on neighborhoods, providing learning and connecting opportunities for strangers to become friends in safe places.

All the while, the ministry of nearly every church in the area has not changed in two decades. The implications of social change for ministry are *huge*, but too few churches recognize the needs or opportunities when they present themselves.

Jesus, the master teacher, laced his teaching with metaphors and illustrations that the crowds would understand. To farmers he spoke about seeds and vineyards, and to city dwellers he illustrated his truths with stories about debt and the justice system. It's a basic tenet of Christianity, but one that is often overlooked. Because the gospel and so many central truths will never change, churches tend to do the same things the same way year after weary year. Then, suddenly, after forty years of doing the same things, they realize that their community has changed completely from what it was and that the church has lost touch. When the church remains the same while the community changes, the church almost always declines—and a declining church is giving up ground in the war to reach the lost and transform the community for Christ.

Barrier #5: The Barrier of Presentation: A Breakthrough of Excellence

Bill was the drama director at First Baptist Church. He did his ministry well, and about once a month the drama department at the church helped illustrate the pastor's teaching with a humorous and relevant sketch. The congregation loved it, and even those who attended the traditional service—at first skeptical of the idea—grew to love these "slice of life" illustrations.

Pastor Sam was thrilled with how the drama ministry was shaping the teaching and vice versa. He watched his congregation's eyes light up each time there was a drama, and he knew that if the drama team could pull together something longer for Christmas weekend, the church could make a huge impression on its members and, more importantly, the streams of visitors. He set Bill to work on a twenty-minute modern-day Christmas drama.

After the show was cast, the entire team went to work blocking and memorizing the piece—except Steve. Steve was a member of the church who worked at the local grocery store as the assistant manager. His hours were long, but his schedule was consistent, and he could make all the rehearsals. Tuesday nights weren't the problem—but his attitude was. Steve had always been a key participant in the short monthly skits, but he didn't seem to be giving any extra effort to the Christmas drama. The deadline to have all the lines memorized was November 15, but Thanksgiving came and went, and Steve still hadn't learned his part. When other drama team members teased him about it after the rehearsal on December 10, he said something about the drama being "only for church" as he got in his car. One member remarked, "Only for church? What does that mean?"

Five days before the production, Steve still didn't know all his lines, and although he wasn't playing the main role, his character was central to the production, and several key lines depended upon the precise timing of his dialogue. Bill, the director, had never tried to pull off a twenty-minute drama, especially not during the best-attended service of the year, and his blood was boiling. Pastor Sam came to observe a rehearsal a week before Christmas weekend, and he could clearly tell that the show was not coming together because of Steve.

When Bill and Steve met the next night, Steve talked about how he would memorize his part "when the time came" and not to worry. "Besides," he said several times, "it's only for church. It's not a big deal. It's not like we're getting paid to get this job done. It'll work out fine."

Steve was right—and that was the problem. Steve learned his lines most of the way, and his timing was mostly correct, and the drama didn't embarrass any of the church members or their guests. In other words, the drama was fine. Not excellent or compelling, but simply fine. It was "good enough for church," as Steve kept saying, and he wasn't "getting paid" to make it any better. The impact of the drama on the community that Christmas season was negligible, and over the next few months several families that had been thinking about visiting that church after the Christmas service decided that the church was just a bit too hokey and unprofessional.

Unfortunately, Steve's attitude is pervasive in the church. Unchurched people have come to expect (but not accept!) mediocrity whenever they attend church. Christians are thought of as copiers, second-rate imitators of secular drama, music, and oratory. Even worse, churchgoers have come to expect *and* accept mediocrity when it comes to presentation-oriented ministry. Few people have the guts to stand up and say, "This is bad. God is not pleased with us offering the leftovers of what we could offer him." God is pleased with sacrifice, with excellence, and with the best we can offer. Consider this warning from Malachi: "'When you offer blind animals for sacrifice, is that not wrong? When you sacrifice lame or diseased animals, is that not wrong? Try offering them to your governor! Would he be pleased with you? Would he accept you?' says the Lord Almighty" (Malachi 1:8).

Sometimes this lackadaisical attitude is held even by the church staff! If that is true in your church, then the road ahead for you is long and hard. If your staff accepts mediocrity because key players are unwilling or unable to expect or deliver better, then those players must be retrained or replaced. You cannot accept a mediocre staff any more than you can afford to accept a mediocre presentation each weekend. This isn't about being "nice" to someone who's "always taught the children's story" even though he isn't competent, or about "not wanting to step on someone's toes" just because she's been singing earplug-worthy "special music" since two pastors previous. It's about ensuring that your church's impact isn't compromised by *any* factor short of an individual seeker's considered decision to go elsewhere. Paul calls the cross a stumbling block, but that doesn't mean the public face of our churches should be one, too.

Excellence in your weekend service presentation is critical to your success in taking new ground for the kingdom. I believe most churches need to narrow their targets of excellence. For most churches today, these three excellence targets are essential for weekend services: excellence in teaching, excellence in worship and musical presentation, and excellence in children's ministries.

People are attracted to and stay at a church because of excellence in one or more of these top three areas; they simply must have the utmost priority for your entire fellowship. The dark question that few churches have the guts to ask their people is this: "Would you be more likely to invite your unchurched friends and neighbors to our church if the presentation in one or more of the top three areas were improved? Does our mediocrity prevent you from inviting someone to church?"

Ought doesn't cut it anymore. Telling someone that she ought to come to church won't budge her from her Sunday routine, but presenting an excellent worship service that touches the heart, stimulates the mind, and engages the soul will break through the barriers of heart resistance. Paying attention to the excellence of specific ministry needs (children's ministry, first impressions ministry, and age-graded programming) demonstrates your commitment to reaching people.

Sometimes a church fails to offer an excellent, well-rounded presentation on the weekends because it is trying to do more than it can do well. Obviously, our goal is to do everything well, but I challenge you to first focus on doing fewer things with excellence rather than on doing more things poorly. As you establish a foundation of excellence, people will naturally be attracted to, and remain at, your church, and the resulting growth can fuel the growth of even more excellent ministries.

Barrier #6: The Barrier of Follow-Through: A Breakthrough of Faithfulness

Susan recently became the volunteer assimilation coordinator of her local church. The pastor asked her to find out what had happened over the course of the past three years. Many people had visited St. Peter's during that period, but few had stayed. Also, some people who had been relatively longtime attendees had started to curtail their involvement, and Pastor George was afraid of what that might mean.

Susan developed a team of five people who began systematically calling visitors who had not stayed at St. Peter's. Over time, they discovered a pattern that shocked them. Even though St. Peter's had always considered itself a friendly church, many visitors shared a similar story. The official greeters warmly greeted them at the door. However, in each and every case, no other person spoke to them. The visitors left feeling that St. Peter's was not really a warm and friendly place and were consequently hesitant to return.

After about fifteen calls with similar results, Susan presented her results to her pastor. In the meantime, George had spoken to several of the longtime attendees who appeared to be detaching from the church. As it turned out, they had a similar experience. Many of those who were lessening their involvement at St. Peter's told a story about feeling that they "no longer fit" and that they were not "insiders" anymore but increasingly felt like "outsiders."

After prayer and conversation, George and Susan concluded that St. Peter's had a problem with cliques—a problem that simply could not be tolerated if the church was to be healthy.

The apostle Paul wrote, "Let us not become weary in doing good, for at the proper time we will reap a harvest if we do not give up" (Galatians 6:9). Paul had it tough: he traveled around as an itinerant missionary, planting churches right and left. He had to leave those churches in (sometimes) trustworthy hands, and then he had to sit in jail and hear horror stories about how bad things had gotten—once he even heard that a man sleeping with his stepmother was affirmed and accepted by a church that Paul shepherded and loved! How much worse could it get?

Yet Paul apparently knew what he was doing when he wrote, inspired by the Holy Spirit, for us not to grow weary, not to give up. Perhaps Paul needed that truth for himself as much as the Galatians did, and one can picture him weeping (or possibly banging his head against his cell wall) as he dictated that sentence. Ministry is hard work. Not giving up—that is even harder. And the difficulty is compounded by the fact that we need to continually examine our mission, evaluate our church systems, and expand our willingness to follow a God-sized vision—even when it involves questioning and changing "the way we've always done things."

During World War II, Corrie ten Boom was a young woman who felt called by God to save Jewish people from the Nazi death camps. One dark night in occupied Holland she prayed this prayer: "Lord Jesus, I offer myself for Your people. In any way. Any place. Any time." [16] God used Corrie in amazing ways that she previously never thought possible as she ministered to hundreds, if not thousands, in her hometown of Haarlem and in the concentration camp where she eventually was imprisoned. What can you accomplish in your local church if you pray the same prayer?

God, by the power of his Spirit, is able to sustain us through hardships we never thought were possible to survive, with our faith intact. He is able to comfort us, give us peace, and strengthen us during the dark moments. Corrie ten Boom experienced this when she and her sister were thrown into a concentration camp. Scripture also repeatedly challenges us to persevere, to hold on, to run the race, to triumph. So in Scripture we find a both/and phenomenon surrounding the reality of perseverance: that there are sustaining factors through the Spirit and that there are choices to be made by us as individuals. Both are in the equation, and both are necessary to "not become weary in doing good." For George and Susan, the work of doing good began with humbling themselves and looking honestly at what their church was really like. That led to the harder work of changing the way they did things, even if it meant ruffling some feathers, because their eyes were fixed on the prize of God-sizing the church for the glory of God.

Once you know the right thing for your vision, your leadership, your community, take a page from Nike and just do it! Do it again and again. Do it well. Do it right. Do it consistently and faithfully. Persistent execution of your vision will produce a harvest. Practice continuous improvement, and be a laser beam rather than a shotgun. A shotgun approach is usually tempting to us since it makes a lot of noise and produces an immediate response from our people. But the laser beam approach will be quieter and more exacting and will yield results worth waiting for.

It has been my experience that staying the course and breaking through leadership barriers relates to four specific dimensions; each of them requires constant attention and poses strategic questions:

1. *Call*: Are you clear about God's call on your life, your call to ministry, and the vision he has for you and for those you shepherd?

2. *Character*: What are the essentials of heart and mind that make up the "you" that you want to be? What is the epitaph you want written on your tombstone by your family, your friends, *and* your adversaries? Are you clear about how your character has been shaped and is shared with others?

3. *Community*: Do you have anchor relationships in your life? Are there people into whom you have invested and who keep you accountable and can undergird your life during a storm? All ministry flows out of relationships. Are you building a community of relationships that model and contribute health in your life?

4. *Competency*: Have you identified your gifts? Are you continuously improving your kingdom effectiveness with your gifts? Are you spending the majority of your time working out of your strengths and doing what you do best, while surrounding yourself with other leaders who complement your weaknesses?

Perseverance in ministry always relates to clarity of vision *and* persistence in follow-through. In short, knowing what to do and doing it right every time! Basically, there are two ways to grow a church: "We must bring people in the 'front door,' and we must keep people from going out the 'back door.'" [17] This process takes time, energy, and more effort than you will have on some days. But never give up, for our God is faithful, and he is able to do immeasurably more than all we ask or imagine.

Leadership barriers are real, but they need not defeat us. Whichever of the six barriers is currently blocking our growth—lack of clear vision, lack of confident leadership, lack of team unity, lack of community connection, lack of excellence in presentation, or lack of faithful follow-through—we can, by the grace of God, break through. Take heart, and grip tightly to your God-sized vision for your church. Then step up to the plate, and do what needs to be done. The reward for leaning into a God-sized vision for your church and ministry will be worth the risk!

chapter 10

GROWTH BARRIERS FOR SMALLER CHURCHES: UNDER 200

As we have seen throughout this book, the number of people attending your church is not the only quantitative manner in which to evaluate your ministry impact. A God-sized ministry always seeks to produce personal, family, and community change to the glory of God. However, several barriers have been observed in churches related to the number in attendance and the corresponding size plateaus. God-sized churches are aware of these barriers and successfully navigate the challenges they present.

Now that we have examined six leadership barriers—barriers that exist in the mind, the heart, or the gift mix of the church leader or leaders—we'll turn to the growth barriers, which are qualitative factors that limit quantitative progress. I often use the following sizes to describe numerical plateaus in church growth:

Descriptor	Average Attendance
Very small	0–99
Small	100–199
Medium	200–399
Large	400–799
Very large	800–1,999
Mega	2,000+

Of all these barriers, the two hundred barrier is the most notable—85 percent of churches in North America stay below it. The dynamics that relate to this barrier are mostly predictable, and from a leadership perspective it marks the quantitative divide between small churches and medium churches. Every size grouping of church has unique factors and makeup, referred to here as its DNA. Each size grouping also has its own size constraints. In the next few chapters we will gain insight into the most commonly referenced growth barriers.

The average church in America has seventy-five participants in worship on Sunday morning, according to "The National Congregations Study" from Hartford Seminary. [18] Approximately 94 percent of churches in America have fewer than five hundred people in worship each week, according to the same study. In this chapter, we will examine the specific leadership challenges for those leading congregations with fewer than two hundred people in weekend worship.

Virtually all the challenges relate to how the pastor and the people understand the role of the pastor. If you are a pastor of what we are labeling a smaller church, you will recognize many issues addressed here, such as expectations of leadership and ways to grow existing leaders and develop new ways of thinking about your role. My prayer is that you will hear a fresh call from God about how to help your dear people become part of God's plan to reach more for Christ in your community.

In light of the large number of small churches in the United States, one might think that people have *chosen* to cluster in small churches because of specific benefits, including intimate and tightly knit community, a "small-town feel" where it's easy to know what others are doing and what they are learning, and spiritually close relationships.

However, some churches are small through no choice of their own. Perhaps their communities are small or declining in population. Over time cities and towns change, and in many parts of the country, the small community is the norm and not the exception. When the number of people is small because of external factors, including the reality of social change—for example, declining population or economic disruption—the challenge is to make the church a healthy and wholesome environment for maximizing spiritual growth. [19]

For many churches, however, the two hundred barrier is unrelated to the size of the community or to economic or social issues. Many small churches are intentionally small for social reasons, not spiritual reasons. I would challenge those of us who lead small churches to carefully determine whether external factors have kept our churches small, or (as I suspect) we have made the intentional choice not to reach more people for personal and social reasons. We do not find biblical mandates for small churches anywhere in Scripture, and time and time again believers are charged with the task of unending outreach. Sadly, some small churches are small because the members want it that way—because it is comfortable and familiar and manageable—regardless of the biblical imperative for outreach.

Furthermore, in most small churches, the staff and lay leaders perform so many tasks that many of those tasks fall outside their primary and secondary spiritual gifts. The net result is a group of believers serving in ministry roles where they are not equipped to serve, leading to frustration, mediocrity, and eventual burnout. If you look closely at a warm, tightly knit small church, you will find a lot of tired leaders doing ministry in areas they do not enjoy, performing tasks they are not meant to do. Pastors and leaders of these churches must cooperatively learn to focus their energies and efforts on what will best enable them to fulfill the Great Commission, rather than on what will keep their small flock comfortable and unchallenged.

Congregation Mindset

The two hundred barrier is often caused by several converging factors, some of which are easy to identify and correct.

Small congregation can have a "small" mindset—and they might even consider "small" to be a spiritual value. Some think that larger churches are not godly because if they are attractive to many people, they must not hold sufficiently high standards. When a church draws crowds, then it is occasionally seen as a secular success instead of a strategically effective ministry. As we have already seen, however, this is far from a universal truth about large churches. To the contrary, many people attend larger churches because the service is done with excellence and laypeople can serve in their areas of giftedness and experience. My goal in this conversation is for all of us not to make assumptions about either form of ministry relative to spiritual health.

Many small-church attendees enjoy the fact that they all know and love one another, and they hold tightly to their right to vote on everything. A more difficult issue to pinpoint is the struggle with the potential sin of pride by some small-church congregants. Some people have a strong need to be known and loved, and they cannot get that attention and status in a larger church. Strong leadership will be needed to ensure that a biblical focus on the Great Commission is part of every church, regardless of the absolute size of the ministry.

Leadership Qualities and Choices

Many pastors of churches with fewer than two hundred people choose to herd sheep instead of herding shepherds, which is also known as sheep ranching. Small-church pastors who want to God-size their churches must accept the responsibility to provide excellent *systems* of care rather than the personal (and impossible!) burden of providing *all* the care to *all* the people. Although some choices are based directly on the congregation's expectations to be pastored directly by the pastor whenever it needs her, at other times these choices reflect what the pastor expects from her leadership.

Pastors are tasked to equip the saints for the work of the ministry (Ephesians 4). Many pastors choose to overburden, and thus limit, themselves by doing all the tasks of ministry themselves, rather than equipping others to minister in their areas of giftedness. For example, one specific task that most pastors should not be doing is pastoral counseling. If pastors are to have the time and energy to truly equip others for ministry, then lay leadership should handle much of the counseling load. How much more impact could the church have for God's kingdom if people received counsel from someone who had the spiritual gift of discernment, rather than from the senior pastor, who might not even possess this gift in counseling situations?

Pastors of smaller churches also continually fall into the manager's trap of micromanaging different ministries instead of letting go of the leadership reins and releasing ministry. Small failures will inevitably happen with this strategy, but major successes will be won when people are mobilized and receive the call to do ministry in the trenches. Let's return to our sheepherder versus sheep rancher distinction:

Sheepherder Pastors
   personally do *all* the caring
   attempt to meet *all* expectations
   work to the limit of their time and energy
   keep work close to themselves
   base perspective on present conditions

Sheep Rancher Pastors
   ensure high-quality pastoral care
   set expectations for others
   perceive the church organizationally
   delegate and involve others
   develop leadership and management skills

Rather than continue to limit their impact, pastors need to empower others to share in the shepherding.

Church Polity and Infrastructure

The organization and structure of small churches can act as barriers to their growth. In many small churches, people hold on to their right to vote on church matters as if their salvation itself were at stake. There are several concerns with this approach. When certain churchgoers lack the biblical knowledge, understanding of truth, and conviction in the evangelical mandate, they cannot be expected to help direct a church toward a strategic vision. Second, you simply cannot lead a church by committee. If it is really difficult to plan a large party with a committee full of people with different ideas and agendas, then why do we expect a church to be led well by scores of committees? Each church should develop a small team of gifted leaders who have passion for the ministry and can help lead the church family. Even in a congregationally governed church family, it is my experience that the church family wants to follow people with great hearts and great passions; it is up to us as leaders to equip and release people for these roles.

Furthermore, smaller churches do not have the infrastructure to add any people to the system, and if more people were added, many systems would collapse. A helpful exercise for your ministry setting would be to list your weekend service attendance in every area of your ministry (large-group service, children's classrooms, adult classrooms, etc.). Now, add two hundred people to the system—or double the number of every single group in every room. Is there capacity? Is there enough adult supervision? Are there enough chairs? Each one of these questions will raise challenges; solving these challenges equips your church and leadership to grow by forcing new and creative solutions. This discipline will produce creative results and thinking outside the limitations of the normal process.

Finally, consider these three classifications of church infrastructure: relational, ministry, and leadership.

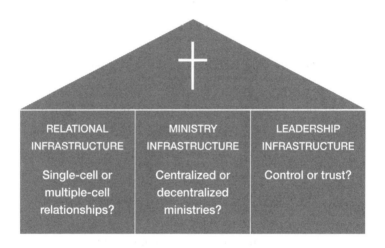

These three categories of infrastructure affect the church at its core by creating barriers in the following ways:

1. Single-cell vs. multiple-cell relationships. Many small churches are made of single-cell groups that relate to the pastor of the church. Larger churches over the two hundred barrier have multiple cells of people groupings that interrelate to each other and the leadership of the church.

2. Centralized vs. decentralized ministries. Ministry over the two hundred barrier takes place in a decentralized fashion as ministries are delegated, activated, and evaluated with trust.
3. Control vs. trust paradigm. Smaller churches tend to favor control over trust (or at least what can feel like unbridled freedom), while larger churches favor trust over control (choosing to risk giving their key people freedom to operate and giving up the structural controls that might be required in a smaller setting).

Developing Barrier-Breaking Strategies

Author and church leader Bill Sullivan, in his excellent book *New Perspectives on Breaking the 200 Barrier* (Beacon Hill Press, 2005), has developed a ten-step strategy that will help you break through the two hundred barrier

1. Examine your motive: Why do you want to stay where you are? Do you want to grow?
2. Intensify your praying: Have you been praying for growth?
3. Increase your faith: believe that God can and will grow your fellowship.
4. Set a barrier-breaking goal: write down on paper a specific numeric goal.
5. Think through your plan: What are its strengths? What are its weaknesses? Show your plan to a large-church pastor for feedback and insight.

6. Focus on the critical few: Which leaders under you are critical to the growth's success?

7. Create excitement: build momentum through testimonies, energy, hope.

8. Launch a growth thrust: be specific and strategic.

9. Evangelize first: focus on the biblical mandate to preach the gospel.

10. Lead the change: change things about your own leadership style and choices, and show by example that you are willing to change, too.

This list helpfully establishes a practice of personal reflection followed by several steps of strategic plans and activities.

Carl George and Warren Bird, in their helpful book *How to Break Growth Barriers* (Baker, 1993), have also put together another list of ideas that can help you break through the two hundred barrier:

- Exude a contagious desire to grow: this flows from the top down.

- Articulate and enhance existing growth factors.

- Take next steps from sheepherder to rancher: start spending more of your time leading the leaders in your midst.

- Deal with institutional factors inhibiting growth: change issues that are preventing growth from happening.

- Resist returning to a small-church mentality: do not cater to self-serving pew warmers who only care about themselves.

- Establish a network of lay-led small groups: move the pastoral-care functions of the church into a small-

group network where people can be known and loved
by believers other than the pastor.

This list encourages a careful examination of culture and basic philosophy of ministry. These values have to be examined, taught, and experienced over time.

If you are the senior leader of a ministry seeking to break through the two hundred barrier, you must be willing to do what it takes to lead your people into God's vision for outreach in your community. There may be some losses along the way as you change the way your church functions—and perhaps the way it has functioned for decades—but the gains for God's kingdom will far outweigh the losses. As you God-size your church, you will see lives change for his glory!

chapter 11

GROWTH BARRIERS FOR MEDIUM CHURCHES: 200–399

O f all the growth barriers that pastors will face, transitioning from what we are calling a medium-size church to a large-size church is perhaps the most difficult. Recent research from Dave Olson of the Evangelical Covenant Church in America suggests that larger churches are growing because of their services, while smaller churches are growing because of their intimacy.[20] Midsized churches, then, may be unable to deliver either extreme. They are too big to be small and too small to be big.

However, difficult doesn't mean impossible. Breaking through the four hundred barrier involves leadership training, multiple entry points, and the pastor becoming a contractor rather than a carpenter. Allow me to explain.

Most pastors in America were trained as carpenters: we understand hands-on ministry and working in direct contact with people, just as a carpenter works directly to shape pieces of wood. Once a church grows to between 150 and 200 people, however, it is impossible for one person to keep up with the pastoral demands of the church congregation—which is precisely why most churches are unable or unwilling to grow beyond that number.

In order to reach more people, the pastor and the people will have to agree about the role of the pastor. Moving from being a carpenter to a contractor means the pastor will see his or her role from a management and organizational perspective, managing several carpenters rather than doing all the work alone. Using the construction analogy, it is the job of the contractor to manage the various subcontractor disciplines and provide what they need to complete their tasks.

Invariably what happens at this stage is one or more crises. I have provided a brief description of these crises and recommendations about how to navigate them.

Crisis of Identity

Churches between two hundred and four hundred in weekend attendance struggle more with identity than any other barrier. "Who are we now?" and "What were we then?" are typical questions. When the church was smaller, it felt as if everyone knew everyone else. (By the way, this was never true. However, since it is true in the mind of the speaker, to deny its reality is typically not helpful!) Now that the church has grown, it can often feel like a mass of strangers. This feeling is accentuated by multiple services and the attendant parking or space problems and people feeling disconnected from any core identity as a church. Pastors leading ministries emerging into this size must ensure that the mission, vision, and values of the church are clear and consistently repeated across the contexts of ministry and ensure that healthy small-group environments exist for care and nurture.

There are two other helpful tools. First, honor the history of the church. Those who grapple the most with feeling a loss of identity are typically those with historical roots in the church. Honor them by linking the current growth with the historical vision of the church. Second, provide at least a couple of events during the year where all church members can gather if they choose to do so—like outdoor picnics or combined worship celebrations—and provide ways for your leadership core to consistently connect with each other. When the people in the church feel connected to each other, they are more likely to trust the direction the church is heading and welcome new members. When the core leaders feel connected to each other, they will be willing to pay the price to accomplish the vision and cultivate loyalty from the people in the ministry who are following them.

Leadership Crisis

When a church grows to between two hundred and four hundred people, there can be a crisis in leadership. The senior leader can no longer meet the totality of pastoral needs—and during that transition he must simultaneously equip others to do much of the ministry for which he was previously responsible. This can create a difficult transition period as the key leader switches roles personally and struggles to meet the expectations of people at various stages of spiritual maturity.

Further, a leader at this size church must have the freedom to try new things and experiment with different ways to reach people. Most typically, the church has a leadership team combining paid and unpaid persons who will serve in staffing roles. My experience consulting with churches at this level indicates that the vast majority of leaders are ill equipped to lead teams of people (see my book *Leveraging Your Leadership Style* for a basic primer on team leadership). Training for your key leaders, whether they are paid or not, as how to lead teams and cultivate team success is a key factor for leadership success at this level.

Finally, the senior leader at this level must embody the leadership maxim "Speed of the leader, speed of the team." A leader who promotes values that he does not personally live out will soon find himself with questioning followers who doubt the heartbeat of the senior leader.

Multiple-Service Crisis

The physical challenges of growth most often lead churches to offer additional services. The practical benefit of holding at least two services is that it makes room for nearly twice as many people in the same space, as well as affording people multiple options to attend and to invite friends. In addition, it provides the opportunity to expand the ministry volunteer work force without requiring workers to miss worship, since they can work at one service and attend another.

However, a move to multiple services often strikes at the heart of what many fear in a growing church. What happened to the "smaller feel" of church as it used to be? How will attendees ever see everyone together all at once? The simple and most direct answer is the most difficult: they won't. The painful truth is that a church reaching more people for Christ will have to sacrifice the comfort of having everyone in one place at one time. (Again, this never really happens, but it is the perception of people, so it is pointless to argue it.) The benefit is that the church can be God-sized and reach all those whom God has entrusted to the church. Our comfort is never more important than the Great Commission.

Crisis of Power

Over the years I've discovered that many church leaders have a deeper commitment to the form of church government with which they have grown accustomed than to the missional function that governmental structure is intended to fulfill. I come from a Baptist background, and my experience is that church fights over church government are far more prevalent than church fights over doctrine and theology.

The way past this crisis of power always lies in a biblical vision for ministry. Pastoral leaders walking with their people through this season of change will need to help people find what is nonnegotiable in their experience with Christ and his church. *How* we do something in church should always be subservient to the *why*. Once people grasp that concept, they can move toward changing the governmental structure to ensure the fulfillment of the vision—and the Great Commission—rather than the continuity of the structure itself.

It was my great joy, while in my early twenties, to work with several long-term church members on the board of my second church. In that church, I learned a very valuable lesson that served me well in later denominational and consulting roles. Most people—yes, I know there are exceptions!—really want their church to succeed in reaching their community. God-sizing church leaders cultivate a culture of passion for the Great Commission and the Great Commandment while leading people to prioritize missional function over governmental form.

Change Crisis

A final leadership crisis in a church of this size involves the process of change. Like the human body, which has only a certain capacity for change—which is why our bodies can go into shock when there is too much loss of blood—organizational systems can react poorly to change. In many of the preceding crises discussed in this chapter, the root issue is change itself. Leaders who help their churches move past this growth barrier will learn to navigate the change process. Part of the change process involves being able to assist people in connecting their experiences of the past with the hope of the future. A good leader will help bring images, analogies, experiences, stories, and *people* from the past of the church into the present in order to help lead into the future.

I remember well the day when I discovered it. The "it" was a tape recording made about thirty years earlier of the church's senior pastor speaking. This particular pastor had been the pastor when the current fifty- and sixty-somethings were in their formative, newly married years. That pastor had later died while serving and was revered by the older generation of the church. (In fact, they named the prayer chapel after him, which is about the closest thing you get to being canonized in a Baptist church.) In the recording, the pastor shared a vision for church planting. I listened to it and made very specific notes. Then, by acknowledging and reflecting that revered pastor's vision, I was able to cast a contemporary vision for church planting that honored both the past and the pastor. The church was able to maintain a heartbeat for church planting from that time forward!

Leadership in and through crisis is the reality of ministry in medium-size churches. Pastors who are called to this setting will experience the hand of God as they effectively lead their people to embrace their God-sized potential for ministry. Each crisis—each barrier to growth—will be met with health and life as people are affirmed for their gifts and the church family prioritizes the Great Commission and Great Commandment in the strategy, structure, and systems of its life together. If God is calling your medium-size church to grow, he will also give you the strength and grace and wisdom to make that vision a reality—a God-sized reality!

chapter 12

GROWTH BARRIERS FOR LARGE CHURCHES: 400–799

Being a leader in a church serving more than four hundred people each weekend is difficult because it means confronting internal and external challenges. A church of more than four hundred people is *clearly* too big to be small, but in many ways it is still too small to be big. Most basic programs will be in place, but being able to deliver an excellent ministry in each one is a significant challenge that can exhaust the volunteer resources and tax the paid staff.

The ministry can no longer be controlled by any one person, or even any five people, and this means that the senior leader must begin to think and act differently in order to break through the next growth barrier. The key word for this barrier is *delegation*, and the key principle is *structure*. The pastor must become a leader of leaders, who in turn lead other leaders, rather than the hands-on, day-to-day manager. Bill Easum said it well when he titled one of his books *Sacred Cows Make Gourmet Burgers*

(Abingdon, 1995). In a church of this size, leaders must be willing to kill some sacred cows—such as programs or ministries that have outlived their effectiveness, or organizational structures and dynamics that are no longer effective—and organize ministry differently in order to reach more people for Christ.

I believe that the two hundred barrier presents key leaders with a barrier of *heart*: Do we have a vision to reach unchurched people? The fundamental question for churches at that level is whether they really care about reaching and transforming people who are lost without Christ. In contrast, the four hundred barrier presents a barrier of *behavior*: Are we willing to change the way we structure the ministry and life of the church in order to reach more people? Ministry at the four hundred barrier requires the pastor to raise up key team members who direct specific program ministries. For the pastor, this will often mean not only delegating responsibility, but also being secure enough to allow other leaders to have significant leadership influence without the micromanaging control that is natural to many pastoral leaders. This letting go will require developing structures to ensure that the church's mission, vision, values, and priorities stay in alignment. Pastors who lead these churches must learn to develop skills in managing people and projects.

Creating multiple program opportunities for people to connect in relationships and serve in ministry is essential to breaking through this barrier. Most churches understand the importance of having ministry on the weekends for worship, children, and students. Developing midweek ministries for discipleship, small groups, and local and global outreach will provide venues to connect people in relationships and give them an opportunity to serve.

For many churches, the specific changes that are required at this level relate to bureaucracy. Will your church be willing to streamline the decision-making process and empower people to serve where they have passion and vision? During my time as a denominational leader, I interacted with a good number of churches that had long-established procedures and barriers that made serving in their churches more difficult than getting top-secret security clearance! Invariably when I asked leaders about those procedures and barriers, they were shocked at my perception—most often because they had not thought about the procedures for years.

Leaders in churches reaching more than four hundred people must prioritize equipping key leaders for ministry. Learning to delegate both power and authority is a fundamental part of this journey. It is a well-established maxim that when someone is given responsibility for a task, he or she should also be given authority to accomplish it. We understand this in our everyday work experience, but we violate it all the time in church. We ask people to accept responsibilities within the church but then don't give them the authority to accomplish the task. This can be as simple as giving the church account number to the person you task with "refreshing" the toys in the nursery, or as complex as ensuring that a person who is given leadership over a ministry activity is given the freedom to accomplish her role using her respective strengths.

The biblical story of Nehemiah is instructive here. As soon as Nehemiah had a vision for rebuilding the wall of Jerusalem, he knew that he needed not only to understand the vision (goal), but also to gather the resources and necessary permissions. Thankfully, all Nehemiah had to do was to get permission and letters of credit from the king—he didn't have to file a single building permit or pass inspection!

Your church can reach more people for Christ, connect them in relationships, and equip them to serve if the senior leaders can surmount the barriers we have discussed in this chapter. Are you willing to change the way you do ministry and make decisions for the sake of engaging more and better-trained people in the process of ministry? The God-sized impact of your church will dramatically increase if people are connected in relationships and serving in ministry. It's a funny thing: the more you give ministry and leadership away, the more your staff and people grow and become God-sized.

As churches become God-sized, there is every chance that they will grow through the four hundred barrier as they reach and retain people in the surrounding communities. In my experience however, the next barrier (that of reaching beyond eight hundred people per weekend service) is made increasingly difficult for a variety of reasons: demographics, campus size, and so on. However, there are some churches in which God begins to move in special ways, churches that reach beyond the eight hundred barrier.

For those ministries, there are numerous difficult questions (and answers!) of evaluation that will determine their willingness to reach even more people for Christ. In my experience as a pastor and consultant, reaching more than two hundred people and reaching more than eight hundred to one thousand people are the two most gut-wrenching times in the life of a church, seasons when hard questions must be faced. While a church between four hundred and eight hundred people is the hardest size to manage, moving beyond eight hundred people each week is the most difficult barrier of evaluation and questioning. Many times people have asked me, "Aren't we already reaching enough people? It is too crowded here already. Can't we stop growing?" I also remember having several conversations with staff leadership about the prospect of reaching more people, which simply meant more work.

At the point of recognizing the costs of reaching more people, we once again have to return to the reason we are doing all we are doing. It is *not* about numbers, it is *not* about acclaim, and it is *not* about fame. It *is* about the Great Commission and impacting people and families for the glory of God. The cost is worth it in terms of life change, family impact, and community transformation.

Of course, as we've seen over and over, God-sizing is about more than numbers. Growing churches must ask hard questions about the sort of harvest their programs and activities are producing. Sometimes all the activity produces nothing more than rising numbers on an attendance chart. If, however, your church is being blessed by God, is reaching more people, and is seeing changed lives for his glory, most likely, your church has asked and answered these tough questions:

- Do we *expect* that every human being can and should become a fully devoted follower of Jesus Christ?
- Are we *intentional* about doing all that we do in light of our size and our community environment?
- Are we *relevant* as we present the gospel? Are we addressing the longing that people have to feel understood, to understand, to belong to something, and to find hope?

- Are we *high quality* in what we present through teaching, worship, and training?
- Do we offer a broad range of attractive *choices* in a variety of areas?
- Do we *trust* our staff and lay leaders?
- Do we ask if a decision was *good* instead of asking *who* made the decision?
- Do we operate from an *abundance model* in which "resource demands" are met by challenging people to find creative solutions?

In addition to asking tough questions about what we do and how we do it, churches that reach and influence more people for Christ often must change the way they organize and carry out leadership at the governance level. Governing boards in churches that are just arriving at this level tend to manage committees, and those committees coordinate volunteers. They also tend to protect physical assets of the church and possess status as lay leaders.

However, in order to make an effective transition to the next level, the governing board of a church reaching more than eight hundred people will release the ministry to the staff (paid and volunteer) leaders of the ministry, who in turn lead growing teams of lay ministers. The governing board of the church then is largely responsible for establishing a climate of trust, authenticity, and support for the vision of the ministry. They help govern the life of the body in such a way as to focus primarily on health, not mechanics. [21]

An additional barrier for churches reaching and influencing more people is the area of staffing. The staff must make several transitions to move to the next level. The staff must move from provider to arranger of service,

from player to coach,

from solo star to team leader,

from privilege to accountability,

from area specialist to age-division generalist, and

from committee appraisal (faithfulness) to
results (fruitfulness).

Each change will require the leadership to provide structures and process to ensure that the staff and the other leaders receive feedback about their respective ministries. Many times, at these levels of growth, the question arises about the proper role of paid staff. In a larger, growing church, paid staff should do the following:

- Communicate mission, vision, and values. This is typically a primary role of the senior leader.
- Manage the church's systems. This can be done by the operational and program staff (paid or unpaid).
- Lead problem solving. Part of the role of ministry leaders is to remove barriers to people serving in ministry.
- Build relationships. Establishing the environment of relational health is a key role of the paid staff leadership.
- Create new opportunities for ministry. Ephesians 4:11–12 is our primary mandate here.
- Perceive the membership in terms of lay-led teams.
- Develop, disciple, and mentor new leaders.
- Train leaders in three areas: spiritual and relational vitality, core competencies, and change management.

Each of these skill areas will help the church be stronger and healthier.

- Have a clear method and curriculum for teaching leadership.

The challenges for this level of church remind me of Hercules battling the multiheaded Hydra: multiple issues can attack at once, and you can never let down your guard. Fortunately, in the latter part of the twentieth century and the first part of the twenty-first century, God has given us a number of healthy larger-church models that we can now both celebrate and observe after one or more decades of ministry. Utilizing other models for ministry as benchmarks—but always remembering that ministries cannot simply be copied or cloned—growing churches can clarify their vision and focus their future in concert with God's hand upon their ministry.

Breaking through growth barriers at all levels does not depend on the mechanics of ministry. Ultimately, the direction of a ministry rests completely in the hands of the Holy Spirit, who calls, shapes, and gifts the members of the ministry team. It is my prayer that your journey toward God-sizing your church will be one that breaks through barrier after barrier by the power of God and for his glory.

Are you beginning to believe God for greater impact than your church has ever experienced? Are you beginning to believe that God can change the trajectory of your church from stagnant and declining to growing and God-sizing in your community? Even now, I hear the walls falling down!

You were made for such a time as this. God has equipped you and called you for this moment. My prayer is for his highest and best as you lead your teams into the future and see and seize what God has in front of you. When you stand in front of the mirror in the morning and when you stand in front of the Master at the end of the age, it is my prayer and belief that he longs to have you hear the words, "Well done, good and faithful servant; enter into the joy of your Master!" That is my prayer for you as you God-size your church!

chapter 13

SO, YOU WANT TO START A GOD-SIZED CHURCH?

Maybe you are not serving in an existing church, or maybe you have a few years under your belt as an associate, and now that you've read all about a God-sized church, you'd like to start one. How would that work?

I believe that there are countless ways God gives people dreams to start new churches. I have often coached church planters, and I am always amazed at the different paths by which God has led them to the task. Even now I am coaching a church planter who came from a conservative evangelical background and has felt led to start a church with a sacramental and some-times charismatic Anglican fellowship.

Thankfully, there are many helpful resources for starting a church. Two of my favorites are *Launch* by Nelson Searcy and Kerrick Thomas (Regal Books, 2007) and *Planting Missional*

Churches by Ed Stetzer (B & H, 2006). I have written elsewhere[22] about the eleven-step process that we have used with many church planters and in our own experience. I want to share these steps with you in the following pages. This is a tremendous step of faith for you and worthy of all the God-stirred excitement you feel. If you are up to the challenge of planting a church, you are in for the journey of a lifetime!

Step 1: Uphold a Clear, Well-Processed, Prayed-for Vision

This vision has to be prayed through and shared in painstaking detail with successive groups of people who will join your team. Because God-sized churches reach large groups of people early on, it is essential to have a clear vision that you know comes from the throne of God (review chapters 2 and 5 for additional heartbeat challenges to developing the vision that God has for you). If you don't have a clear idea of what to do with the crowd when it comes, you will be in trouble!

There are some tremendous resources on the market to help you develop your action plan. Five of my favorites are *Purpose Driven Church Planting Materials* (www.saddlebackresources.com, search for "church planting"); *Dynamic Church Planting* (Paul Becker, www.dcpi.org); *Church Planter's Toolkit* (Bob Logan and Steve Ogne, Church Resource Ministries, www.crmleaders.org); *Planting Thriving New Churches* (Ray Johnston, www.baysideonline.com); and, as I mentioned a moment ago, *Launch* by Nelson Searcy and Kerrick Thomas (www.churchleaderinsights.org).

Step 2: Lay Out an Aggressive Plan of Action, including a Fund-Raising Plan

When I coach prospective church planters, they tend to underestimate the amount of money that will be required to successfully plant a God-sized church and to overestimate the amount that a denominational agency, mother church, or sponsor should be obligated to give them at launch. If you are the leader of a God-sized church, people you have influenced in ministry will support your vision. Raise funds from those who buy in to your vision based on God's working in their lives.

Fund-raising is a challenge for many pastors and church planters. Most pastors are hesitant to speak about money, and most church planters want someone else to raise the money while they do the ministry. But a God-sized church leader must have the ability to cast a compelling vision and be the lead fundraiser for the ministry. In our experience at CVC, we learned powerful lessons in this regard as God worked through our vision casting with various people and agencies.

The apostle Paul certainly knew what it was to have a vision that came from God, yet he still required funds from ordinary people! Read 2 Corinthians 8–9, Philippians 4:15–17, Colossians 1:24–29, and Galatians 1:15–24, 2:6–9 to see the vision that God gave Paul and how he was constrained to raise money to fulfill it.

Step 3: Create a People Pathway for Assimilation

Assimilation at every level revolves around connecting people in relationships and in ministry service. I have found Rick Warren's model at Saddleback Church (www.saddleback-resources.com) to be the most helpful in our setting. In our ten-year history, we have morphed from the base path of the Purpose Driven model to a triangle and now an arc with the circles of involvement where our three primary environments are described (see chapter 6 for additional details). We talk about our three environments as inviting, connecting, and serving. Instead of asking people to remember four, five, or more things, we simplified to these three environments. Articulating a clear plan at the start helped people to have confidence about where we were heading and connecting them in relationships and ministry.

The key process question in assimilation is this: Can you take a new believer through the spiritual journey of discipleship to leadership? It is a critical question for all Christian ministries, and you must have your answer (at least in part) before your church launches. As I shared earlier (see chapter 4), our church has made many mistakes in the process of our growth and life, and after ten years, we are still working to get our systems and process in order.

Step 4: Make Your Church-Planting Plans Flexible, and Be Open to Unexpected Opportunities

We had some great plans on paper! Some of them even worked. Others didn't. We recorded thirteen sixty-second commercials for radio. We got no response. Direct mailing in our area was not nearly as effective as we hoped. But we discovered some strategies that did fit our area. People in our community actually watch local public-access television. Newspaper inserts reach 80 percent of all households in the area. The cost was substantially cheaper than direct mail, and people retained the inserts, sometimes for months.

There may be a God-sized ministry inside you that will be birthed sometime in the near future. My advice would be to use your "expectant" time to the fullest, reading books, consulting experts, and listening to birth stories. Those who have had a part in birthing a God-sized church or ministry usually don't need much prompting to tell their stories. Become involved in a church-planting network, where you can receive coaching, tools, and resources. (Two networks where I am personally involved are Growing Healthy Churches at www.growinghealthychurches. org and Thriving Churches at www.thrivingchurches.com.)

Step 5: Prayerfully Seek Godly Core Leaders and Key Ministry Leaders

Implosion is a critical danger to launching a God-sized church ministry. Churches that attract crowds and don't have the leadership base to effectively minister will be at a disadvantage from the start. Seeking godly core leaders as part of your launch team and cultivating a game plan for how the church will go public with specific ministries are necessary for a successful launch of the God-sized church. Here are several key roles for you to prayerfully pursue:

- a spiritually gifted leader and gifted communicator (may be one person or two)
- a worship leader who can help draw and connect other gifted musicians
- a children's ministry leader/facilitator
- a student ministry leader/facilitator
- a small-group coordinator for adults
- administratively gifted folks for office and ministry support

You could easily become discouraged by viewing this "dream" list. How many church plants fill every single position? The reality is that some people may overlap responsibilities and cover more than one area. But remember that no one person can fulfill all of them, and if you think you're the one, think again. Build a team of people around you, and go for it!

Step 6: Hold Preview Services Three to Six Months prior to Your Launch Service; Build Your Core to One Hundred Adults or More

Many church plants have benefited from the preview service strategy, that is, once each month (for a few months prior to the launch) the church offers a church service in the community. It's best to offer everything you would offer at a weekly service, such as children's classes and refreshments. This process was crucial to our church's early development. During your preview services, you may need to "borrow" key leaders from other churches (ideally a "mother church" or "partner church") in order to provide a basic children's ministry and worship experience. The church planter should speak here and provide a solid teaching that will meet needs (I focused on marriage and parenting in our preview services). During each of these services, you are looking to cast the vision for your church plant and praying that God will help you grow your leadership core. I believe in the power of strategic praying—so pray that God brings you the right leaders and that you see people come to know Christ at each preview service. At CVC, our experience was that people in our existing core got very excited when they experienced God's hand moving among us and that the newer people who became part of the core could point to the preview service as the catalytic experience for them joining us in the journey.

Step 7: Engage People in Ministries, Discovery Classes, Small Groups, and Bible Studies

One of the things that we learned at our church plant in northern Nevada was that if we would offer our Discovery 101 class (our class for new attendees) on the afternoon of our preview service, it would give an immediate way for folks who were looking at the new church to hear more of our vision and plans. Providing easy on-ramps for people to join you in your ministry is essential at all times, but never more critical than at the early part of your new church life. I would also challenge you to make it a high priority to connect people in relationships through small groups and/or serving through ministries. My experience is that if people are challenged by the vision, connected in relationships through small groups, and serving in a ministry, they will be well attached to your church.

Step 8: Identify the Core Group as Your Launch Team, Create Job Descriptions, and Prepare for Launch by Training Your Launch Team

My experience with church plants has been that insufficient leadership resources are a huge potential pitfall. I have personally witnessed many churches begin with a "bang" (an exciting launch) and end with a "whimper" (a final service) within the span of two or three years. I am convinced that one of the keys to preventing this cycle is to ensure that you have a large and broad leadership cohort at the beginning of your church life. Challenge people to know that they are personally critical to the success of the church launch. The Holy Spirit will draw many people to your church launch, but each person who comes is critical to God's plan. Ephesians 4:7–16 teaches us that each individual part contributes to the functioning of the whole body. During this launch phase of the church, the church planter will need to gather partners in ministry and be looking (again, with strategic prayer!) for gifted men and women to help lead the body that God is forming.

Step 9: Create Excellent Publicity, Especially Two Months before Launch

My brother Gene was the marketing whiz behind our church launch. He believes strongly in what I call "bread crumb" advertising. He builds a game plan where over a three- to six-week period we build public interest and drive people to a specific response. Our theme, "The Next Great Day in History," moved people to focus on February 22, 1998. Then the second segment focused on the teaching series, "Winning Big in the Game of Life." Doing this publicity made some people mad; they were members of existing churches—even though we clearly were not targeting current church attendees. We like to say that during this period we took the "flak" in order to build the "flock."

We involved our people in the process by giving them fold-over wallet-sized cards with the name of the church, topic of the teaching series, and the location and times of services and encouraging them to canvass neighborhoods and local businesses and hand out the cards. The expectation is to create a buzz of activity in your area. When we launched, we think we created a big-event mentality. Not only is event evangelism in the center of our vision, but we believe that it is right for our area. The launch of your God-sized church is the most important event in its early life and will determine the trajectory of the next twelve to twenty-four months. We strongly believe that birth weight affects birth health. Although I recognize that some churches launch in a more organic way (utilizing small relational networks), what I provide here will be of great help to those establishing a church with a high attractional component.

Step 10: Plan a Super Launch, and Go Public with the Key Things You'd Die For

You can't control everything. Mistakes happen. Weather may be stormy. People get sick. But you can decide what you are going to the wall for. CVC decided to focus on three things:

1. Relevant biblical messages
2. Upbeat contemporary music
3. Excellent children's ministry

These three program distinctives remained our weekend crowd focus for the entire time of my ministry in Nevada. If you were to go fishing, you would think about how fish think and what they like to eat. Church planting is about strategic penetration into an unreached culture. My experience (in a North American setting) is that teaching, music, and children's ministry are the three key elements that most people look at *if* they decide to even visit a church. So, my counsel is to at least focus on these three areas as you prepare to launch your church.

Step 11: Go for It! Affirm Philippians 4:13 and Practice Continuous Improvement

Above all else, finish well! Consider these characteristics of those who have finished well, based on the research and experience of Paul D. Stanley and J. Robert Clinton in their book *Connecting*:

1. They had perspective, which enabled them to focus.
2. They enjoyed intimacy with Christ and experienced repeated times of inner renewal.
3. They were disciplined in important areas of life.
4. They maintained a positive learning attitude all their lives.
5. They had a network of meaningful relationships and several important mentors during their lifetime. [23]

Expectant times are full of nervousness, stress, and a need for clear thinking. You may be in a significant "expectant" time of ministry now, or you may see one in your near future. Either way, my challenge to you is to seize the moment and learn as much as you can. When it happens, take a lot of pictures, record your memories, and share them with others who hope one day to birth their own exciting ministry.

God is sovereign. It is his church. You are accountable for gifts and resources he has entrusted to you. But he is the one who causes the growth. God will do way beyond your imagination, and you will see a thirty-, sixty-, or hundredfold return from the sowing of his seed. Spend time affirming your leadership team. Be a positive person from the platform, and practice continuous improvement. Build a culture of affirmation and expectation, and go for it! If there is a God-sizing vision within you, God will help you build the ministry that he has placed inside your heart and mind.

chapter 14

THE RIPPLE EFFECT:
GET OUT OF LINE—IT'S WORTH IT!

K im and Carol found us when we were not even an
official church. They were lapsed Lutherans who had
seen an advertisement for an event we did a few weeks
earlier and decided to check us out after the big event. We were
meeting in a casino ballroom, forming a core group for the eventual church launch. On the day they attended, our core group
was doing its first baptism of twelve people. The baptism took
place in the back hallway of the casino ballroom in a garage-sale
hot tub. We had filled it with water directly from the hot water
heater, via 150 feet of garden hose trailing down the hallway and
into the kitchen, so steam rose in thick swirls as it hit the air
from the twelve-degree weather outside, racing its way up the
stairwell from a door that someone had left open on the first
floor. Kim's response to all this?

"People this crazy for God are people I want to be around."

Two years later, with their family growing in faith, one of Kim and Carol's daughters invited her friend Casey to be part of a children's choir we started. After a few weeks of Casey's participation in the choir, her parents, Curt and Laura, thought they better find out what this church was all about. Curt was a nonbelieving Catholic, and Laura was a lapsed Baptist. On the way out after the service, Curt headed toward me with a determined look. I thought, *Oh, man, I'm in trouble.* What I didn't tell you is that Curt is a former NFL lineman. He's big! He hugged me (I still thought I was going to die) without saying anything and walked out the door.

The second weekend they attended, he came to me with that same look, but this time with tears in his eyes, and he said that he had "prayed the prayer" and asked Christ into his life. Laura rededicated her life to Christ as well.

Those decisions were made about seven years ago. Today Curt and Laura are still active at LifePoint Church and have invited many other friends who have made decisions for Christ. Curt has been involved in developing sports ministry, video for weekend services and special projects, and many other forms of outreach. Laura has served in our communications ministry for the past several years and as our communications director. Both continue to inspire lives every week for the cause of Christ. And all of this God-sized changing began with a simple visit of Kim and Carol to a casino hallway.

So, is it worth it? Is it worth all the risk, all the challenge, all the uncertainty?

Yes! The power of God to change lives never wanes. Mike Breaux wrote the book *Making Ripples* (Zondervan, 2007) based on a sermon he preached. When I first heard the sermon, Mike shared the wonderful image of a pebble dropping in a pond, sending ripples from the point of initial impact outward. The kingdom of God works the same way. The power of God touches a life. Then that life touches another life and another life, and the kingdom of God breaks into our families and communities and workplaces.

I believe in the power of God to change not only a human life, but also a church. A church that becomes God-sized will influence its community in ways that are ultimately measurable only in eternity. While I believe this with all my heart, the truth is that the challenges are huge. I agree with Robert Lewis when he says:

> As the church engages a third millennium, it . . . looks across a terrifying—and ever-widening—chasm:
> Between first-century authority and postmodern skepticism;
> Between a bold proclamation of God's love and unmet human needs;
> Between the selfless vision of Christ and the self-obsessed reality of our world;
> Between the truth of God's laws and the moral compromise of our culture;
> Between those who believe and those who don't.[24]

As church leaders, we simply must face that chasm with an unshakable conviction that the church is the hope of the world when we present the good news of Christ in relevant and accessible ways to men and women whose hearts are far from him. The church *is* God's solution.

Robert Lewis also challenges church leaders to become "bridge builders" and connect the church with the community—this is the core hope I explore in my book *Pastorpreneur.* Lewis knows that a bridge builder is about making a God-sized impact in the world through transformed and mobilized people: "A 'bridge builder' has a vision to raise the lifestyle standards of his people and move his church off its island setting into a city or community. He crafts strategy, builds structure, and measures success, not in terms of size or programming, but in terms of authentic witness, influence, and impact in the community at large." A bridge builder instinctively knows that "a church's health is measured by its sending capacity, not its seating capacity." [25] This is why I have stressed over and over that God-sizing isn't a numbers game—it's about transforming as many lives as we can through the power of God and for his glory.

This book, *God-Size Your Church,* has been an invitation to dream big dreams for God—and to begin living and leading in the land of those dreams, watching them become realities. There are formidable dangers in the land, to be sure, and they are not to be underestimated. Church ministry is a war; we must don armor, and there will be casualties. But we can have courage, because he who called us is faithful. Ultimately, there is no safer or more joyful place to live than in the center of God's big dream for you.

We are excited to see your church thrive and your dreams grow for his glory! If God is birthing in you a heartbeat for a God-sized ministry, then we'd love to hear from you! If you go through the process of starting a high-impact church, we'd love to hear the story of how God works in your vision to produce a harvest that is thirty-, sixty-, or hundredfold. You may write me at john@thrivingchurches.com; we'd love to hear your story!

Included in the appendix are documents that might be helpful for your ministry. Some of them are from the early days in CVC's church life and represent the very basics when we started the church, while others represent very recent realities. No matter where I serve, we try to keep growing and improving our ministry. However, if you can use these resources and improve them for other church planters and leaders, please do so and share the improved versions with us!

We are yours for the kingdom. Seeing a life change, transforming a family, and inspiring a community for the cause of Christ are worth the investment of your life. A God-sized church will change lives for all eternity . . . including yours!

APPENDIX

Bylaws of the Carson Valley Christian Center, Inc.

This church shall be known as the Carson Valley Christian Center, incorporated under the laws of the State of Nevada.

Purpose

Carson Valley Christian Center (CVC) exists to see non-Christians become disciples of Jesus Christ.

Carson Valley Christian Center will dynamically

. . . exalt Jesus, the Light of the World

. . . equip believers to walk in the Light

. . . encourage one another to share the Light

Statement of Faith

We have chosen to use the masculine pronoun throughout the doctrinal section of this document for ease of language, but our intent is to describe both genders, not the male gender exclusively.

Scripture

We believe that the Bible is the Word of God, fully inspired and without error in the original manuscripts, written under the inspiration of the Holy Spirit, and that it has supreme authority in all matters of faith and conduct (2 Timothy 3:16–17).

The Trinity

We believe that there is one living God, and that He has revealed Himself in three distinct persons: God the Father, God the Son, and God the Holy Spirit (Titus 3:4–6).

a) God the Father: We believe in God the Father: an infinite, personal spirit, perfect in holiness, wisdom, power, and love. We believe that He concerns Himself mercifully in the affairs of men, and that He saves from sin and death all who come to Him through Jesus Christ.

b) God the Son: We believe that Jesus Christ is fully God and fully man. He is eternal and shares all of the attributes of deity with the Father and the Holy Spirit, as God's only begotten Son. He was conceived by the Holy Spirit to be born of a virgin, Mary. We believe in His virgin birth, sinless life, miracles, and teachings. We believe in His substitutionary atoning death, bodily resurrection, ascension into Heaven, perpetual intercession for His people, and personal, visible return to earth.

c) God the Holy Spirit: We believe that the Holy Spirit is a person and shares all the attributes of deity with the Father and the Son. He came forth from the Father and the Son to convict the world of sin, righteousness, and judgment, and to regenerate, sanctify, and empower all who believe in Jesus Christ, and that He is an abiding Helper, Teacher, and Guide.

Salvation

We believe that all men are sinners by nature and by choice and are, therefore, deserving of eternal condemnation. We believe that those who repent of their sins and trust in Jesus Christ as Lord and Savior are regenerated and become children of God by the Holy Spirit (John 1:12; Romans 5:6–8).

The Church

We believe that the Church is the Body of Christ, of which Christ is the Head. It consists of all regenerated persons. We believe in local churches as visible manifestations of the invisible Body of Christ, the Church Universal. We believe that God has given the task of evangelism of the world to the Church under the direction of the Holy Spirit and the Word of God (Acts 1:8; 1 Corinthians 12:12–14; Ephesians 1:22).

Christian Living

We believe that a Christian should live for the glory of God and the well-being of others. Believers are called to live holy and godly lives (1 Corinthians 10:31; 1 Peter 1:5–6; Matthew 22:37–40).

Ordinances

We believe that ordinances of the New Testament church are communion (the Lord's Supper) and water baptism for believers by immersion as a public act of confession of faith (Acts 8:36–39; 1 Corinthians 11:23–26).

Last Things

We believe in the personal and visible return of the Lord Jesus Christ to earth and the establishment of His kingdom. We believe in the resurrection of the body, the final judgment, the eternal joy of the righteous, and the endless suffering and separation of the lost (Acts 1:11; Isaiah 9:6–7; 2 Peter 3:7; John 3:16).

Christian Liberties

We believe in the personal lordship of Christ over individual believers. Each believer must give account for himself to Christ. Therefore, in matters not strictly defined in Scripture, convictions of one should not be imposed on others (Romans 14).

Article 1: Membership

Section 1: Membership and Requirements

Membership in the church family is open to those who meet the following requirements:

a) Profession of faith in Jesus Christ as Savior and Lord.

b) Completion of membership class requirements as outlined in church ministry documents.

A list of members who are actively participating in church ministries will be maintained.

Section 2: Dismissals

Membership may be terminated in the following ways:

a) Member initiates request for membership termination.

b) The Elders may remove a person's name from membership after appropriate efforts to restore fellowship and participation have failed. There shall be no time limit, but shall be up to the discretion and good judgment of the Elders.

c) The Elders may dismiss a member as part of a disciplinary action.

Section 3: Annual Meeting

There may be an annual meeting of the membership. The place, date, and time of the annual meeting will be announced in public worship or in print two weeks prior to the meeting. The annual meeting, when held, will be for the purpose of consideration of any ministry matters appropriate for the membership to consider or of modification of the Bylaws.

Article 2: Government

Section 1: The Headship of Christ

The government of CVC will seek to maintain the lordship and direction of Jesus Christ as the Head of this Body. Those in authority will continually seek His mind and His will, through His Spirit and His Word in all actions and decisions.

Section 2: The Board of Directors

The Accountability Team will serve as the corporate Board of Directors of the church. As such they will seek to support the ministry of the church by precept and example under the lordship of Christ and through the leadership of the Pastor. They will pray together regularly and review the progress of the ministry.

They will gather together for prayer and counsel on a regular basis, at least monthly. Members of the Accountability Team will be selected by a majority vote of the members then serving.

Subject to the limitations of the Articles of Incorporation, other sections of the Bylaws, and of Nevada law, all corporate powers of the corporation shall be exercised by or under the authority of, and the business and governance affairs of the corporation will be managed by the Directors. Without limiting their general authority, the Directors shall have the following authority:

a) To select and remove all other officers, agents, and employees of the corporation; prescribe such powers and duties for them as may or may not be inconsistent with the law, the Articles of Incorporation, or the Bylaws and fix their compensation.

b) To conduct, manage, and control the activities and business of the corporation; and to make rules and policies not inconsistent with the law, Articles of Incorporation, or the Bylaws.

c) To borrow money and incur indebtedness for the purposes of the corporation, and for that purpose to authorize to be executed and delivered, in the corporate name, promissory notes, bonds, debentures, deeds of trust, mortgages, pledges, or other evidences of debt and securities.

Section 3: Elders

In addition to Directors, the church will have a Pastoral Staff who serve as the Elders of the church. These men will meet biblical qualifications and are responsible to shepherd the spiritual health of the church family.

To be selected as an Elder, a man must meet the qualifications outlined in Scripture in 1 Timothy 3:1–7 and Titus 1:5–9.

There will be a minimum of at least two and no more than fifteen Elders. Additional Elders may be added by the procedure described below. Elders will be nominated by the Pastor and a majority vote of the Elders then serving.

An Elder, other than the Pastor, may be removed from office by the vote of a majority of the Elders then serving. The Pastor may only be removed by a two-thirds (2/3) majority vote of the voting membership of the church present at a meeting called in accordance with Article 4.

Article 3: Officers of the Church

Section 1: Officers

The officers of this corporation will be a President, may include a Vice President, and a Secretary and Treasurer. The Directors may also appoint other officers as they may deem necessary. No person, other than the President, may hold more than one office.

Section 2: Election

The Directors shall elect by simple majority vote the officers of the corporation from their number at the first meeting of each year. The term of office is to be one year, or until their successors are elected and qualified.

Section 3: President (Pastor)

Subject to ratification of the Board of Directors, the President shall have general supervision, direction, and control of the business and activities of the corporation. He shall be responsible for the presidency of all meetings of the membership, Elders, Directors, and shall have other powers and duties as may be prescribed from time to time by the Directors.

The primary ministries of the Pastor are to be the lead visionary, teacher, and equipper. He will give himself to the ministry of the Word and prayer. He will teach, guide, and lead the church to fulfill the vision for ministry that God has entrusted to him and to this Body. As President, he also serves as the Chief Executive Officer of the Corporation and Chair of the Elders. He is responsible to supervise and provide direction for any other staff and/or ministries of the church.

In the event of a vacancy in the office of President (Pastor), the Elders shall develop a committee to search for a successor Pastor. Once the right candidate is found (either within the Body or from outside candidates), the candidate will be presented to the church membership. A 75 percent vote of those voting members present (with at least a quorum of 30 percent of the voting membership present) will be required to elect a new President.

The Pastor is to be compensated by written agreement with the Directors. Compensation, benefits, and expenses provided will include (as God supplies the resources): housing allowance, salary, health insurance, retirement, continuing education, and other reasonable ministry expenses. The written agreement is to be reviewed no less than annually.

If a termination of the Pastor is to be considered, it requires the call of at least two Elders to initiate a meeting of the Elders. The meeting shall be called in accordance with the procedure for establishing a special meeting. Should three-fourths (3/4) of the Elders then serving concur that the Pastor should terminate his pastoral leadership of the church, the matter will be brought before the voting membership at a duly called meeting. A three-quarter (3/4) majority of the voting membership (with a quorum of 30 percent of the voting membership present) will be required to terminate the pastoral ministry.

Section 4: Other Ministerial or Support Staff

The Pastor may present other ministerial or support staff to lead the ministry to the Accountability Team for their advice and consent. Each staff person so presented will have a job description containing duties and compensation reviewed by the Accountability Team. All staff members serve under the Pastor's direction and supervision, and at his pleasure.

Section 5: Vice President

In the absence or disability of the President, if the organization has a Vice President, the Vice President shall perform temporarily all the duties of the President, and in so acting shall have all the powers of the President until the Directors take action on the vacancy. The Vice President may have such other powers and perform other duties as may be prescribed from time to time by the Directors.

Section 6: Secretary

The Secretary shall keep a full and complete record of all the proceedings of the Directors; shall keep the seal of the corporation and affix it to such papers as may be required in the regular course of business; shall make services of such notices as may be necessary or proper; shall supervise the keeping of records of the corporation; and may have other such duties as prescribed by the Directors.

Section 7: Treasurer

The Treasurer shall receive and safely keep all funds of the corporation and deposit them in the bank or banks that may be designated by the Directors through the administrative staff of the church. Financial procedures, as indicated in these Bylaws or in policies adopted by the Directors, shall be followed in the disbursement of funds.

Article 4: Financial Support and Fiscal Year

This church shall operate on a calendar year from January 1 through December 31. This church shall be supported through the tithes and offerings of its members and friends.

Article 5: Miscellaneous

Section 1: Execution of Documents

The Directors may authorize by majority vote any officer or officers, agent or agents, to enter into any contract or execute any instrument in the name of, and on behalf of the church and such authority may be general or confined to specific instances. Unless so authorized, no officer, agent, or other person shall have any power or authority to bind the church by any contract or engagement or to pledge its credit or to render it liable for any purpose or to any amount.

Section 2: Inspection of Bylaws

The church shall keep in its principal office the original or a copy of its Articles of Incorporation and Bylaws, as amended to date, certified by the Secretary, which shall be open to inspection by the members at all reasonable times during the office hours.

Section 3: Construction of Definitions

Unless the context otherwise requires, the general provisions, rules of construction, and definitions contained in the Nevada Nonprofit Corporation Law shall govern the construction of these Bylaws.

Section 4: Rules of Order

The rules contained in Robert's Rules of Order, as most recently revised, shall be the general guide to govern all business and/or Board meetings of the church, except in instances of conflict between said Rules of Order and the Articles of Incorporation and Bylaws of the church or provisions of law.

Section 5: Dissolution and Nonprofit Status

The property of this corporation is irrevocably dedicated to religious purposes and no part of the net income or assets of the organization shall ever inure to the benefit of any Director, officer, or member thereof or to the benefit of any private person.

The Directors shall make a recommendation regarding dissolution to the membership; said action to be approved by a two-thirds (2/3) vote of the membership. On the dissolution or winding up of the corporation, its assets remaining after payment of, or provision for payment of, all debts and liabilities of this corporation, shall be distributed to a nonprofit fund, foundation, or corporation which is organized and operated exclusively for religious purposes and which has established its tax-exempt status under section 501(c)3 of the Internal Revenue Code.

Section 6: Liability

No officer, Director, Elder, or representative appointed by this church shall be personally or individually liable for any error, mistake, act of omission for, or on behalf of this church, occurring in the scope of his or her duty as such officer, Director, Elder, or representative, excepting only for his or her own willful misconduct or violation of law.

Article 6: Amendment of Bylaws

These Bylaws may be amended or repealed and new Bylaws adopted by the membership of the church at a properly called meeting. Amendments shall be provided to the membership upon recommendation to the Accountability Team. Adoption of amendments or new Bylaws shall require a three-fourths (3/4) vote of the membership.

Ministry Program Leaders Expectations (updated 05/07)

Periodically it is important to clarify basic expectations for our ministry together. I have written elsewhere about how subministries (basically, everything but the weekend service) get developed and led with excellence. For those of you who give leadership within a ministry area, I thought you should also know the five key things that I expect every ministry area to do:

1. Understand and communicate the CVC mission and vision. Our mission is "Reaching unchurched people to become disciples of Jesus Christ," and our vision is "The spiritual transformation of Northern Nevada and the Mountain West through the power of Jesus Christ." *Nothing* at CVC (including me!) is above that mission and vision . . . the vision drives and directs *everything* at CVC. If that vision is not being fulfilled through an activity, then kill it and get going with something that does fulfill the vision.

2. Create an environment where the vision can be fulfilled. We have three primary kinds of environments at CVC . . . *inviting environments* where people can experience God and come to know Christ as Savior and where we can invite and bring our friends to meet Christ, *connecting environments* where people can connect their hearts to God and to one another in authentic relationships, and *serving environments* where people can discover and utilize their SHAPE (Spiritual Gifts, Heart/ Passion, Ability, Personality, Experiences) for serving on campus, in the community, and in the world.

3. Make sure that ours is an environment where people are counted because people count! End of discussion. I can't live with subministry environments where we don't know who participates, whether they are consistent in attending, or whether we've seen them in the last few weeks (or months!). Someday, we'll even get to the place where we can do a good job with "knowing" the crowd/curious on the weekends. But the congregation, connected, and core *must* be counted. See definitions below.

4. Foster an environment where relationship values get lived out. LifeTeams, in all their varied forms, simply means that we create an environment where people are known, challenged to grow, and healthy spiritual habits are encouraged. In the end, I know with absolute certainty that if our people don't develop a biblical foundation/worldview, experience authentic relationships, and discover their SHAPE, then they will *not* be "fruit that remains . . . ," and we will have failed in our vision to create disciples.

5. Lead a team of people who are doing ministry, leaders of others who are doing ministry, and developing leaders of leaders. Over time, CVC will rise or fall based on leadership . . . because everything rises and falls on leadership! I've often used the "carpenter, contractor, architect" analogy with staff members. Each ministry area should have "first serve" places where people can step in and do *something* to help them connect and begin to find their gifts (carpenters). Every ministry should be developing leaders who can oversee others doing the ministry (contractors). Each ministry should also be passionate about identifying, growing, and releasing ministry to high-capacity volunteers and equipping leaders who are leaders of leaders (architects).

CVC People-tracking Definitions (5/07)

Community . . . Anyone we've had contact with and who gave us his or her name and address. We cull this list once a year.

Curious . . . These are folks who are periodic attendees at CVC, but to our knowledge have made no commitment to Christ and are not plugged into anything at CVC.

Congregation . . . These are folks who are attendees at CVC, but other than participating in some activities are not plugged into a small group or serving at CVC

Connected . . . These are members and regular attendees who are involved in a small group and/or are serving in ministry at CVC, with an understanding of the mission/vision/values of CVC. To the best of our knowledge they are striving to lead a Christ-centered, biblically grounded, heart-sensitive life.

Core . . . These are members (people who have completed 101-201-301) who are committed to the mission/vision/values of CVC and can communicate those to others, are involved in a small group, are serving in a ministry role, and striving to live a Christ-centered, biblically grounded, heart-sensitive life.

CVC Values

1. Evangelism occurs primarily in relational contexts in family, work, neighborhood, and community settings and secondarily in outreach events that are easily accessible to seekers.
2. God's Word is consistently and relevantly taught in corporate worship, small groups, classes, personal discipleship, and through creative activities.
3. Performing arts are honored and utilized to the glory of God in a fashion relevant and accessible to seekers.

4. Community life in the church family is so honored that division and gossip are confronted quickly, clearly, and resolved in accordance with biblical principles of fellowship and conflict resolution.

5. Spiritual gifts discovery and utilization are essential aspects of discipleship for every believer.

6. Ministry programs and activities are started, led, and grown by gifted men and women from the church family.

7. Support ministries are led by people with serving gifts. These people are regularly honored and affirmed.

8. Pastoral staff model ministry values of team, affirmation, and excellence through their teaching and relating with the church family.

9. We honor those God has gifted and called to authority. Those in authority exercise their leadership with humility and grace as servant-leaders.

10. Stewardship of God's financial resources is practiced, modeled, and taught with passion and clarity.

NOTES

1. George Barna, *The Second Coming of the Church* (Nashville: Word Publishing, 2001), 1.
2. Great Commission Research Network (formerly the American Society for Church Growth), http://www.ascg. org/index.htm.
3. C. Peter Wagner, presentation at Fuller Theological Seminary, circa 1983.
4. See www.perrynoble.com.
5. Walt Kallestad, *Turn Your Church Inside Out* (Minneapolis, MN: Augsburg Press, 2001), 12.
6. Vision Cycle graphic copyright © 2003 by Dr. John Jackson. Used by permission. All rights reserved.
7. Gary McIntosh and Glen Martin, *Finding Them, Keeping Them: Effective Strategies for Evangelism and Assimilation in the Local Church* (Nashville: Broadman Press, 1992), 22.
8. Visit www.zipskinny.com, and search for your zip code to compare a variety of factors in your local area.
9. Gary McIntosh and Glen Martin, *Finding Them, Keeping Them: Effective Strategies for Evangelism and Assimilation in the Local Church* (Nashville: Broadman Press, 1992), 132.

10. http://www.brainyquote.com/quotes/authors/a/ alvin_toffler.html.

11. http://quotationsbook.com/quote/30505/.

12. Peter F. Drucker in the foreword of *The Leader of the Future: New Visions, Strategies, and Practices for the Next Era*, ed. Frances Hesselbein, Marshall Goldsmith, and Richard Beckhard (San Francisco: Jossey-Bass, 1997), xiii.

13. Lyle E. Schaller, *The Very Large Church* (Nashville: Abingdon Press, 2000), 107.

14. Carl F. George and Warren Bird, *How to Break Growth Barriers* (Grand Rapids, MI: Baker, 1993).

15. John Jackson, "Help Your Church Grow" (Rev. Magazine, 2004).

16. Corrie ten Boom, *The Hiding Place* (Grand Rapids, MI: Chosen Books, 1984), 74.

17. Gary McIntosh and Glen Martin, *Finding Them, Keeping Them: Effective Strategies for Evangelism and Assimilation in the Local Church* (Nashville: Broadman Press, 1992), 9.

18. Dr. Mark Chaves et al., "The National Congregations Study: Background, Methods, and Selected Results," Journal for the Scientific Study of Religion 38 (1999): 458–76.

19. Several useful resources are available for those leading smaller congregations to health. See resources at www. thrivingchurches.com, www.easumbandy.com, and www. alban.org.

20. Dave Olson, *The American Church in Crisis* (Grand Rapids, MI: Zondervan, 2008).

21. There are a number of excellent resources on this subject. My personal favorites are *Direct Hit* by Paul Borden

(Nashville: Abingdon, 2006) and *Winning on Purpose* by John Kaiser (Nashville: Abingdon, 2006).

22. John Jackson, *Pastorpreneur* (Colorado Springs: Biblica Publishing, 2011). See www.pastorpreneur.com for additional information.

23. Paul D. Stanley and J. Robert Clinton, *Connecting: The Mentoring Relationships You Need to Succeed in Life* (Colorado Springs: NavPress, 2006), 215.

24. Robert Lewis, *The Church of Irresistible Influence* (Grand Rapids, MI: Zondervan, 2001), 23.

25. Ibid., 177.

BIBLIOGRAPHY

Barna, George. *The Second Coming of the Church*. Nashville: Word, 2001.

Borden, Paul. *Hit the Bullseye*. Nashville: Abingdon Press, 2003.

———. *Direct Hit*. Nashville: Abingdon Press, 2006.

Breaux, Mike. *Making Ripples*. Grand Rapids, MI: Zondervan, 2007.

Collins, Jim. *Good to Great*. New York: Collins, 2001.

Cordeiro, Wayne. *Doing Church as a Team*. Ventura, CA: Regal Books, 2005.

Easum, Bill. *Sacred Cows Make Gourmet Burgers*. Nashville: Abingdon Press, 1995.

George, Carl, and Warren Bird. *How to Break Growth Barriers*. Grand Rapids: Baker, 1993.

Jackson, John. *Pastorpreneur*. Colorado Springs: Biblica Publishing, 2011.

Jackson, John, and Lorraine Bossé-Smith. *Leveraging Your Leadership Style*. Nashville: Abingdon Press, 2006.

Kaiser, John. *Winning on Purpose*. Nashville: Abingdon Press, 2006.

Kallestad, Walt. *Turn Your Church Inside Out*. Minneapolis, MN: Augsburg Press, 2001.

Lewis, Robert. *The Church of Irresistible Influence*. Grand Rapids, MI: Zondervan, 2001.

Maxwell, John. *21 Irrefutable Laws of Leadership*. Nashville: Thomas Nelson Publishers, 1999.

McIntosh, Gary, and Glen Martin. *Finding Them, Keeping Them: Effective Strategies for Evangelism and Assimilation in the Local Church*. Nashville: Broadman Press, 1992.

O'Neill, Tip. *All Politics Is Local*. Holbrook, MA: Adams Media Corporation, 1994.

Osborne, Larry. *The Unity Factor*. Vista, CA: Owl's Nest, 1989.

Rusaw, Rick, and Eric Swanson. *The Externally Focused Church*. Loveland, CO: Group Publishing, 2004.

Schaller, Lyle. *The Very Large Church*. Nashville: Abingdon Press, 2000.

Searcy, Nelson, and Jennifer Dykes Henson. *Fusion: Integrating Newcomers into the Life of Your Church*. Ventura, CA: Regal Books, 2008.

Searcy, Nelson, and Kerrick Thomas. *Launch*. Ventura, CA: Regal Books, 2007.

Stanley, Paul D., and J. Robert Clinton. *Connecting: The Mentoring Relationships You Need to Succeed in Life*. Colorado Springs: NavPress, 2006.

Stetzer, Ed. *Planting Missional Churches*. Nashville: B & H Publishers, 2006.

Sullivan, Bill. *New Perspectives on Breaking the 200 Barrier*. Kansas City, MO: Beacon Hill Press, 2005.

ten Boom, Corrie. *The Hiding Place*. Ada, MI: Chosen Books, 1984.

Tichy, Noel. *The Leadership Engine.* New York: Harper, 2002.

Toffler, Alvin. *Future Shock.* New York: Bantam, 1984.

Warren, Rick. *The Purpose-Driven Church.* Grand Rapids, MI: Zondervan, 1995.

To contact Dr. John Jackson
to tell about how *God-Size Your Church* has impacted you
or to have him speak in your church or at your conference,
e-mail him at john@drjohnjackson.com.

John Jackson is the president of William Jessup University (www.jessup.edu), the co-founder of Thriving Churches International (www.thrivingchurches.com), and the founding pastor of LifePoint Church (www.lifepointnv.com), of which 40 percent of the current attenders were previously unchurched.

John is a fifth-generation preacher with ministerial roots beginning with his great-great-grandfather who was a lay preacher in Great Britain. His great-grandfather was the third member of the Salvation Army, his grandmother was an ordained minister, and his father was a pastor as well. John's primary gifts of leadership, teaching, and administration give him a passion for seeing people come to know Christ and fulfill their Kingdom potential.

John is a graduate of the University of California at Santa Barbara (Ph.D, M.A., in Educational Administration & Organizational Studies), Fuller Theological Seminary (M.A. in Theology/ Christian Formation), and Chapman University (B.A. in Religion/Christian History, cum laude). John and his wife Pamela have been married for over 30 years and have five children ranging in ages from 25 to 11. They make their home in Genoa, Nevada.

ALSO BY JOHN JACKSON

Pastorpreneur equips pastors to employ businesslike strategic planning and innovation skills to enhance their congregational leadership. Jackson's practical strategies and grand vision will empower you to explore new methods for maximum impact on your church and community . . . and become the church that you and God dreamed of.

Paperback, 192 pages, 5.5 x 8.5
ISBN: 978-1-60657-106-4
Retail: $15.99

Available for purchase at book retailers everywhere.

Learning about where you fit in the family of God can be experienced both in relationships with others and in personal reflection. *Finding Your Place in God's Plan* provides teaching, daily devotionals, and small group materials for these purposes.

Paperback, 176 pages, 5.5 x 8.5
ISBN: 978-1-60657-083-8
Retail: $15.99

Available for purchase at book retailers everywhere.

ALSO AVAILABLE

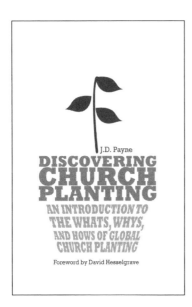

Discovering Church Planting explores the biblical, historical, and missiological principles of global church planting as well as unfolds practical strategies for confronting contemporary challenges to our vital task in reaching a lost world. This comprehensive introduction to church planting shows the reader how to apply effective, international church planting practices to specific contexts.

Paperback, 458 pages, 6 x 9
ISBN: 978-1-60657-029-6
Retail: $22.99

Available for purchase at book retailers everywhere.

While not primarily an apologetics text, *What If It's True?* provides helpful apologetics resources while speaking practically about the impact of the resurrection of Jesus in ordinary life.

Paperback, 128 pages, 5.5 x 8.5
ISBN: 978-1-60657-085-2
Retail: $10.99

Available for purchase at book retailers everywhere.

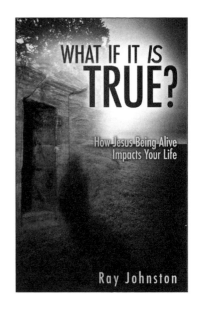